The Dark and Feeling

The Dark and Feeling

Black American Writers and Their Work

By

Clarence Major

The Third Press

Joseph Okpaku Publishing Co., Inc.
444 Central Park West,
New York, N.Y. 10025

Library of Congress Catalog Card Number: 73-83162
SBN 89388-118-X

First printing

Designed by Bennie Arrington

ACKNOWLEDGMENTS

"The Tribal Terrain and the Technological Beast": copyright ©
1974 by Clarence Major. Excerpt titled, "Notes on Writing," first
appeared in *Essence*, copyright © 1971 by Clarence Major. Reprinted with permission.
"The Explosion of Black Poetry" copyright © 1972 by Clarence
Major was first published in *Essence*, June, 1972. Reprinted with
permission.
"The Black Aesthetic edited by Addison Gayle, Jr." copyright ©
1971 by Clarence Major was first published in *Essence*, March,
1971. Reprinted with permission.
"Some Changes, Poems by June Jordan" copyright © 1971 by
Clarence Major was first published in *Essence*, January, 1971.
Reprinted with permission.
"catechism of d neoamerican hoodoo church, poems by Ishmael
Reed" copyright © 1971 by Clarence Major. First published in
Essence, March, 1971. Reprinted with permission.
"Blueschild Baby, a novel by George Cain" copyright © 1971 by
Clarence Major. First published in *Essence*, July, 1971. Reprinted
with permission.
"The Autobiography of Miss Jane Pittman" copyright © 1971 by
Clarence Major. First published in *Essence*, September, 1971. Re-
printed with permission.
"Williard Motley: A Vague Ghost After The Father" copyright ©
1969 by Clarence Major. First published in *Nickel Review*, Oc-
tober 3, 1969. Reprinted with permission.
"Frank London Brown: Reckless Enough To Be A Man" copy-
right © 1969 by Clarence Major. First published in *Nickel Review*,
September 26, 1969. Reprinted with permission.
"Work With The Universe: An Interview with Clarence Major
and Victor Hernández Cruz" copyright © 1969 by *Nickel Review*.
Used by permission of the publisher.
"Interview with Clarence Major" copyright © 1973 by Liveright
Publishing Company. First published in *Interviews With Black
Writers*, 1973. Reprinted by permission of Liveright Publishing
Company.
"Black Criteria" copyright © 1967 by Clarence Major. First pub-
lished in *The Journal of Black Poetry*. Reprinted with permission.
"On Censorship: An Open Letter To June Jordan" © 1973 by
Clarence Major. First published in American Poetry Review, Vol.
2, No. 4, Aug-Sept. 1973. Reprinted with permission.

Contents

Part One

The Tribal Terrain and
The Technological Beast

Eighteen. I was eighteen when I sold my first story and for the following fifteen years I published my work consistently in newspapers and magazines, but I was thirty-three before I dared feel I was beginning to break even and about to make some progress. Eighteen years old. I remember well the day I received the letter of acceptance. I was in a cold town in Wyoming. I see myself now. Walking from the post office, the crunching snow beneath my feet. My bulky parka holding back the free movement of my arms. In my hand, the air mailed letter. My heart beat insanely. I was fearful of opening it, yet I suspected it to be an acceptance. The return address told me who it was from: James Boyer May, Editor of *Trace*, then Guest Editor of an anthology in progress, *Olivant*. My knees felt weak—and even before I read the letter I was sick with joy. My hands shook. And I was freezing. My nose running. Trembling, I knew this item in my hands would fill me with more joy than I felt in years—possibly with more joy than I'd ever felt in all my life! For it would be my first step!

I sat down on the curb of the street, suddenly, unable any longer to endure the mystery; tears were beginning to run down my frozen face from my clouded eyes. In this one earth-shaking moment my dreary life here as a student moved way to the back and far to the side of my conscious experience. I sat there, my ass soaking up the snow, and tore open the letter and read each word slowly. My lips were forming the words and I felt I was tasting their shapes.

11

And I lived on the thin and beautiful and elusive energy of this new food to my ego for a very long time. In point of fact, I *had* to: it was the only staple my spirit had had a chance to ingest. From age twelve, when I first started playing with the notion of writing "seriously", while writing crude little novels in school notebooks, my psyche had nearly starved to death for want of encouragement and recognition. The longing to communicate cannot long survive a vacuum.

Anyway it took two years before the big, handsome orange anthology containing my first story, "Ulysses, Who Slept Across From Me," was published. Seeing my work in print made me more conscious of what I was doing, forced me to a greater sensitivity toward words.

Words. The raw material of my trade and the medium that either bridges or stands between peoples everywhere.

In the summer of 1969 I served as a consultant in Afro-American Literature at Cazenovia College, in Cazenovia, New York. The participants were to be college instructors and professors attempting to ready themselves to teach black literature. Before going to Cazenovia from Massachusetts, where I was then living, I made the mistake of planning *what* I would say to the participants in the project. At the same time I was going with some rather unsatisfying conclusions about the nature of words and the written word.

The first question I asked the participants was, "What is the difference between Black Excellence In American Literature and Excellence In Black American Literature?" The title of the course was Black Excellence in American Literature and none of them had thought about it and none of them could give an answer. But I had two reasons for asking; one, to demonstrate the trap of word games, and two, to suggest an opening to a deeper level of the subject than the ethnic identification promised.

The written word. In the woods of Massachusetts I'd done a lot of thinking about the origin and function of writing. And I had arrived at the unhappy conclusion that, ever since writing made its appearance (perhaps somewhere in and sometime during the fourth and third millenniunm), it had been used to exploit and control people. In any case, it was not directly the result of the neolithic revolution. We know that by now. We also know that humanity, in various cultures, has achieved tremendous force and social progress *without* a single scratch of help from the written word. However, cities—the roots of civilizations—have always been an accompanying reality wherever writing developed. And always writing correlated as one of the main tools for enslaving people. Writing as luxury, as material for art and in the interest of science, too, seems to end with a negatively ulterior motive rather than the goal of enlightenment. Certainly it was not *invented* in the cool and noble interest of spreading the joy of aesthetic experience nor for the purpose of making available scientific knowledge.

In the 1960s there was a crisis of sorts regarding the written word. Many writers, mainly white, expressed either dismay or a downright loss of the impetus to work. This was a time so many of them felt their chosen task was, in some disappointing way, a desperate copout, an activity which had by its nature too little to do with "action" which had become the key word. Some even felt the written word did not lead quickly enough to a means for changing the bad, bad world in which we all live.

The 1960s we know were times of infamous assassinations —one sympton of what might be called the Second Great Turning Point in the Western experience. The first was that dark and bloody moment when Constantine decided to become a Christian, to call together all the dispersed little groups bickering among themselves and to order them to worship one and the same god, a fantastic phallic symbol whose mythological life functions as a riddle in code language. This was Jesus the Christ, who, by the way, was constantly being put to death everywhere he could be found—both in fantasy and in reality. This act attempted to meet the unconscious need to challenge and if necessary destroy the father figure so the male ego could burst forth and make felt its own presence in the world, as man and not boy. The father and son warfare.

13

We all certainly know what Christianity and Judaism, their exchange and conflict, led to—what the energy of both finally helped to do to the Roman Empire. Life after death may have had its great appeal but witch-burning was always for profit and it made the church rich because, and it was not by accident, most of the witches burned were property owners or they possessed material goods worth having, and the belongings of a witch or a devil put to death by the church usually became the property of the clergy.

I had absolutely no doubt that this was proper undercurrent subject matter for the Cazenovia course. The message on the dustjacket of Ishmael Reed's anthology, *19 Necromancers From Now* lends a clue: "Dance and Drums preceded the word. Thousands of years before the invention of the novel or the short story, Thoth, the black Birdman of Egypt, 'invented letters' and 'gave names to things'. Magic/Religion came before 'criticism', and words *(nommos)* were the rappings of not one but thousands of Gods. Centuries before the 'literary capitals' of London, Paris and New York, Ifé in Nigeria was the home of the Necromancers, conjurers of dread and joy./Kidnapped by bandits and transplanted to North America, they became HooDoo men, maintaing the faith of the old religion . . ."

Most of the writers who lost faith in *the word* were white; the blacks among them were few. White writers in North America seemed to have succumbed to the death of the spirit by the end of the 1960s.

By 1970 United States bookstores were flooded with books by black writers and it was no accident that most of the works of fiction and poetry produced by these craftsmen dealt with the search for human fulfiillment or the tragedy of racial crisis. They showed implicitly or explicitly a clear relation to the facets, the historical nature of the outsider as he or she is in any culture's literature where clearly a subculture survived to tell its own tale.

Just as in any so-called "advanced" culture most of the books published are worthless, so, too, a great many of the things published here by black writers were hack material. As always, a few were greatly overrated. Many good writers, in the same stroke, were underrated or completely neglected. But the intellectual possibilities opened by many of these works were vast—possibilities that allow for an assessment of the social and political and moral problems and questions implicit in their contents. If you have the intellectual yardstick to deal with it, it is certainly more fun, less dull, to explore these large, shapeless areas, in works of art where there is color, smell, sound, feeling, in a sense, than to plow your way through miles of abstract verbiage seeking to obtain some vestage of concrete information regarding, say, the forces that produced the "blood pounding" homosexual experiences in James Baldwin's *Another Country.*

As a literary theme, an assesment of the violence, hatred, and frustration in the quest for self-discovery is, like the theme itself, no small matter. One could go into the correlating dramatic power, the lyrical and allusive qualities, the atmosphere, the success or failure of these artistic properties as they relate or fail to relate directly to the subject matter.

So be it. I wanted to suggest to the Cazenovia participants that black authors were whole people who, when they were lucky, produced whole books, works with a rounded sense of humanity. They should seek the sense of humor, if it was there, and the bizarre, absurd or what is often called the "savagely funny" in some of these works by people like Charles Wright and Ishmael Reed and William Melvin Kelley. Why not discuss these qualities in relation to the writer's sense of reality, from the point of view of their *own.* If not a full meal as food for thought at least the idea had a premise as an appetizer.

Just as actors study for years to learn how to deliver a performance that flows naturally, it was finally through the hard work I put into *All-Night Visitors* that I came (in Ralph Ellison's words) "to possess and express" the spirit and to understand *with feeling* the footnotes on who and what I was. This certainly does not mean that *All Night Visitors* is autobiographical. The real point, of course, is that I came into

15

the possession of my own technique—in itself, the single luxury that can either liberate or trap a writer—as a person.

Until around this time I had, in some ways in my attitude toward my work, been both liberated and trapped at the same time. The distinction I had made all along between poetry and prose I gradually realized was and had been a serious trap. For me, at least. It was false and it had been hanging me up. I came to see that what I had been trying to do in making a novel was the same thing I meant to do in producing a poem: to invest the work with a *secret nature* so powerful that, while it should fascinate, it should always elude the reader—just as the nature of life does.

Putting together the anthology, *The New Black Poetry,* gave me a different but equally important kind of perspective. Frankly it was a *job* in the sense that *All-Night Visitors* wasn't. It meant reading tons of bad stuff to find the good. It meant a lot of *thought,* mainly, and the nature of that thinking was primarily the business of decision-making which caused me to consider even more sharply my own work.

In this spirit I found myself making many last-minute changes in *All-Night Visitors.* It was a novel that had come slowly out of the sidestreets of my conscious and unconscious life. It made its tortured way into its final form. I called it an epic collage poem. I felt my madness, though less naive than St. Augustine's, was vividly shown and the beauty of it had to be hyphenated into the possibilities of the reader's mind. I saw the work as a kind of drawing done with words.

At the end of the summer, 1969, the Cazenovia stay over, I began work on the final draft of my novel, *NO.* Before submitting it to the publisher I wrote this explanatory note on the projected work:

In *NO* I am interested in probing deeply and evenly and fully the combination of conscious and unconscious experience.

I mean for the work to create its own terms. It is not meant to be satire. It is realistic work of what we call fiction. Its

16

realism is as real as that middle land between sleep and wakefulness.

And in terms of theme, mainly, I am exploiting a range of taboos, fears, cultural limitations, and social traits, springing from attitudes concerning a wide range of human experience, sexual, racial, historical, national and personal. In *NO* the "spirit" of the narrator's "head" is meant to function both as a "scheme" (plot) and as central force, conveyor of the "story" and a screening device for the development of the work as an entity. The main concept involves demonstrating the plight of Moses Westby's tragic imprisoned birth and growth and ultimately how he transcends this penal system.

The "prison" is spiritual; it is also "physical" and it refers to an area of human activity (in this case largely concerning black Americans) that is as precisely personal as it is political. The logic that the action and ideas depend on is meant to be as *im*plicit as the plot *in* that it is a "secret plan"—as one finds in but cannot quite define in a good poem. This manner of mind and these activities will be both familiar and at the same time, distant, strange; which is, in all of our minds, exactly what the fusion of unconscious and conscious reality amounts to. I am not writing more about the penal system than the people trapped in it.

That statement indicates a very real faith in what I was attempting to do, but that faith had been long coming and it had finally come only when I had gained control of my materials.

It was in this optimistic frame of mind that I stopped work on the novel to go for one day to speak with a psychology class at the University of Rhode Island. The course was called "Being Black"—a classroom experiment in human transactions. My presence was an effort to fulfill what they chose to call a person-to-person confrontation. To warm up I read three scenes from *All-Night Visitors*. Most of the students had already read the novel since it was required reading in the course but many of them felt my reading took the spirit of the work into their minds from a new angle.

Some of the students were concerned with alternatives to what actually happened *in* the novel which led to a discussion of the nature of probability or *if*. My point was that no one was properly equipped to deal with anything other than what *does* actually take place—in the novel or out of it.

Yet such concern remains at the apex of the human will. We are all compelled by our memory of the past and our perception of the present to fix our vision, our desires, our fears, our thoughts, no farther than that area wherein we find concrete terrain, precisely no farther than that very past, this very present. At the same time, what makes up the other end of this paradox is the historical human need *to project* these visions, desires, fears, and ideas onto the absolutely unknown and unknowable nature of the future. And, since there is never any response from the future, we invent answers.

Writing poems and novels is also a way of inventing answers. If you are black and born in the United States and happen to feel the compulsive urge to write, and if you are to have the slightest chance at real success, the style of your inventions, must from concept to finish be dominated by and operate in and through the premise of your racial identity. If you happen to be an American Japanese comedian, you get nowhere unless you tell jokes stemming from your ethnic character.

However the discontented spirit of black people continues to shake up the sluggish mood of America. In this antipoetic, provincial, insular and social-realistic-oriented superculture, the problems which a black writer works his or her way through in getting the work done are in the long run the main problems of civilization—assuming that the work turns out to be real. Black writers today are more urban than white writers. All the white writers have moved to the country and the upsurge of black literature, its vitality, may have resulted in no small measure from this recent development, not to mention all the other more obvious causes. I mean, you have to live in a great city in order to feel the pulse of the time and if you don't feel it the energy of it won't be present in your work. In the earth it is at the point of the most intense pressure that the diamond is created.

Some things become popular and always you have a mob of people doing them. Seems most black critics have decided Ralph Ellison's head is out to lunch. They resent his stance. They say he's too apolitical.

But the Black Literary-Political Establishment is a very curious organization. Hot air at the center, its thrust seems to come in spurts, like that of its white counterpart. Aside from passionately helping white publishers to cultivate blatant mediocrity, many members of the B.L.P.E. go all out to become performers and show personalities in the name of the art of writing. I'm referring to the ones who conduct themselves like comedians. Perhaps they are victims of what Ralph Ellison sees as the sad misunderstanding of the relation between suffering and art.

I think most of the trouble stems from a fear of or disrespect for one's inner life, the unconscious experience, and its interplay with one's conscious life. The social realist can never suggest that "hidden system of organization" because he has never touched it. But it is present in all life and therefore should be in art.

Finally the question of art—or, more directly, the future of black American literature—involves the whole question of human communication. If we are going to point out the direction of black writing, we will have to see it not only in the total context of North American literature (which includes the work of American Indians) but also in a world perspective. We will have to get at the roots, to understand the influences which the very language (English) has on the writer's mind, and also to see how the destiny of black art is bound to the destinies of other peoples. As a result the tribal terrain within each of us may make peace, for the first time in the history of the world, with the technological beast in which we live.

Formula or Freedom

1. The Black Novelist

"A work of art," I wrote recently, "can be a complete thing; it can be alone, not preaching, not trying to change men, and though it might change them, if the men are ready for it, it is not reduced in its artistic status. I mean we black poets can write poems of pure creative black energy right here in the white west and make them works of art without falling into the cheap marketplace of bullshit and propaganda. But it is a thin line to stand on."[1]

Though I am now referring to the novel rather than to poetry I still believe in this principle only more strongly, but I also recognize now that very few people have the nerve or the desire to stand on that difficult line. The rewards are hardly ever material and often not clear and almost never quick. For the black novelist it means earning one's reputation on the basis of one's work and maintaining it that way, not by becoming a Negro leader or amusing the public with political antics. The black novelist who travels the way of art in the United States risks his or her very life.

What then have been the alternatives? Many black novelists have simply conformed. But on what appear to be very strange terms to some one completely outside the situation.

Black folks who *use* their own blackness to "get ahead" (as Robert Boles says in an interview[2]) are unfortunate. True, but then the whole society is unfortunate because we live in

21

a world that lends itself totally to the crude art of exploitation. Anything, every idea or feeling or type of person, can be and often is subjected to interests outside its own essence and beauty. We know the common use of sexy women on TV to sell products, but not many of us are reminded of the renewed movement of black novelists and black and white critics to elevate to a sociological pedestal, once again, the sacred propaganda tracts, produced and manufactured in the interest of the freedom struggle. Every thirty years or so it happens all over again.

Sometimes it all seems very funny. The other day I said to Ralph Ellison, "I'm doing a piece on the black novel and you're in it," and he laughed and replied, "But I'm a Negro." I had to laugh too. But part of our salvation is contained in the fact that we understand and express the humor in what we feel and think. Then the comic sense becomes the finest if not the only way to approach something too terrible to talk about with a straight face.

Somewhere in the question, the mystery of being, is the motive beneath our urge to communicate. The written word evolves from speech and the novel is, among other things, a form of communication. Yet the attitudes brought by both the writer and the reader to novels written by black people make it possible to see these works as a group separate from American fiction in general.

Since the end of the 1960s even more excitement has surrounded these novels than surrounded the Jewish-American novel. Obviously black novels are of a nature that calls sharp attention to the sociopolitical plight of black people. However throughout the thicket of this melee the question of art hardly arises. It seems not to apply to black writers. Black writers who mention art to publishers are laughed at. In any case, the excitement one witnessed around the Jewish-American novel during the 1950s was not of an ethnic or sociopolitical nature because the Jewish writer became an American. All exceptions can be granted but the point is that the question of European-American literary values was usually considered relevant to the Jewish-American novel. In contrast the word "literary" never applied to black writing and many black writers themselves considered the idea of a "literary work" obscene, irrelevant or strange.

In taking a look at black novels and their authors separately from American fiction, in considering their moods and interests, it is clear that black novelists form a distinct group with very clear-cut cultural characteristics peculiar to no other group. But you can't get around the fact: among the black novelists themselves there is so much diversity that *no single* Black Aesthetic or formula or fixed method for looking at their work can be employed. You might do well to employ instead a fresh open mind.

Sutton Griggs' words, "the bird that would live must thrill the hunter with its song,"[3] sadly still apply to much of the effort on the part of black fiction writers today. The often cited "inferior quality" or "impressive mediocrity" of black fiction is due in part to the lusty efforts of publishers coupled with the nearsighted assistance of too many black writers themselves to hustle what they, together, imagine to be the "current" public interest in Blackness. This jive game involving the black writer has been around since William Wells Brown saw the publication of his novel, *Clotel* (1853). As Ralph Ellison says, "we are encouraged to talk about how bad we've been treated, and this becomes a sort of perverse titillation for white people."[4]

As long as the role which publishers and the media design for black writers is acted out, as long as there is no bold challenge to the social network by which the black community functions in its relation to the status quo and the source of white power, as long as there is no threat to any of these areas, the black writer stands a chance at best becoming nothing but a good ole American public figure. James Baldwin got caught in this trap for a while but pulled out. Others gladly remain. But to assert one's individuality—without denying the important link with the black community—and to win status on the merit of one's work, too often means one will be ostracized

23

by both black and white. In other words, to be a black artist is to be unpopular. It is a simple fact of human experience: society protects itself by destroying originality yet it depends on originality for renewal. But if a black novelist does manage to escape, to assert the self, with an original novel, then there is at least a small and more flexible segment of the reading population upon which such a writer can depend to respond in a positive way.

Whether or not you judge a novel by a black writer according to European-American standards or a private Black Aesthetic is a moot point. Several good books come to mind. They are *The Outsider* by Richard Wright, *The Primitive* by Chester Himes, *Night Song* by John A. Williams, *Beetlecreek* by William Demby, *Ladies of the Rachmaninoff Eyes* by Henry Van Dyke, *Hue and Cry* by James Alan McPherson, *The Bluest Eye* by Toni Morrison. In any frame of reference they *should* remain good.

The generation of black novelists who came along after World War I, but before World War II, were mainly driven by the trauma of their social experience to produce novels of bitter protest. The few who managed to find publishers for their works well represent the larger percentage that never reached print. This whole movement reached its peak through Richard Wright, specifically in *Native Son*. Throughout these years hardly anyone dreamed of looking at the novels black writers made without also considering the setbacks and victories of black people in general. After World War II, when there was some indication of integration, "integration" novels began to appear. Most of the authors of these novels had been trained in journalism and they produced, in their social realism, a sort of fictional journalism.

By 1950 black writers still hung up in "protest" fiction began experiencing some difficulty finding publishers for their works. In speaking of protest fiction I am not referring to works like Chester Himes' *If He Hollers Let Him Go* (1945) or William Gardner Smith's *The Last of the Conquerors* (1948); rather, I refer to novels nobody now remembers, such as Lloyd

Brown's *Iron City*. Anyway, Chester Himes, disgusted with the American publishing industry, to say the least, moved to France and started writing and publishing there his famous detective novels. Richard Wright's manuscripts were beginning to meet rejection by one publisher after another. Something new was in the air. You might call it a "revolt against protest." Out of it came Ralph Ellison and James Baldwin.

Ralph Ellison's feeling was, "People who want to write sociology should not write a novel."[5] Meanwhile Ellison's own primary concern was that of any artist: to utilize his roots and racial folklore as material for fiction and to bring to this material all the skill he could manage. But he got caught in the crossfire of the cultural nationalist and the cultural integrationist. However, he was not destroyed: he grew stronger.

James Baldwin, aside from occupying a very large place among contemporary American authors on European-American standards, is, in a sense, the last in the United States' Tradition of One Negro Author At A Time. By this I mean that, even on non-black terms, there are today too many new and brilliant young black novelists—real artists—for the reading public to go on pretending it cannot celebrate more than one black novelist at a time. (That tradition was of course a brutal one: it threw Chester Himes in the shadow of Richard Wright and Jean Toomer in the shadow of Langston Hughes.) Whether or not this white approach to black writers will again become popular remains to be seen. In any case, a new and better educated generation of black readers reduces the importance of such a question. The civil rights movement and the riots of the 1960s and the new black consciousness that grew out of these developments helped, too, to destroy that single-minded white approach to black writers.

The novel *not* deliberately aimed at bringing about human freedom for black people has liberated as many minds as has the propaganda tract, if not more. This does not mean that a wholly human novel by a black writer necessarily becomes assimilable for just anybody. It does mean, though, that a work that takes long root in its author's experience—race being a part of that experience—not only makes sense anywhere in any language but also is likely either to raise hell or to lower heaven.

So in connection with this, those black writers, integrationists or nationalists, who were unaware of their own "complex fate" (in the Ralph Ellison sense) did not in the past and do not in the present deal with and give the reader the wholeness of their own experience. We see evidence of this in some painfully bad novels turned out by black writers, witness Willard Motley's *We Fished All Night* (1951) or Langston Hughes' *Tambourines To Glory* (1958). It is in itself hard enough for any writer to see through the thick surface of things, to select the correct incident, to bring to "life" an assortment of impressions, symbols and ideas, but for black writers, particularly for those whose "complex fate" is submerged in the understandable political interest of black nationalism, it is infinitely more difficult, working in English, a language with a white "personality." The question of how to strike a balance becomes very real—how to maintain a well-rounded view of what is experienced, and, of what is experienced, how to discern what is best internalized for the filtering into the entity that becomes a work of art. These are dead serious questions for dead serious times—not to mention the fifteen years of work it takes simply to learn how to write a novel!

Another part of what I am really getting at is that the individual struggle to create something carries with it a unique set of experiences that usually is not transferable, at least not wholly, and that in the United States, because of the odds against black people, success at any level for the black novelists becomes, in each case, a shining miracle. Little wonder the whole black community renews its broken spirit through the achievements of these few miracles!

Before discussing my impressions of the critic and criticism, and more problems of the black novelists, I would like to indicate further the sort of novels I hold in high esteem, to lend support to this arrangement of ideas. After doing this I would like also to point out another aspect of black fiction—one that

26

bothers me. But first the novels: *Invisible Man* by Ralph Ellison, *The Narrows* by Ann Petry, *Cane* by Jean Toomer, *Giovanni's Room* by James Baldwin, *Many Thousand Gone* by Ronald L. Fair, *Yellow Back Radio Broke-Down* by Ishmael Reed, *The Wig* by Charles Wright, *Curling* by Robert Boles, and, *A Glance Away* by John Wideman. Now for the other promise.

This problematic aspect of black fiction has to do with the puritanical hangups of many black writers. Too many tend to be as antisexual as their white counterparts. So anxious are they to prove that they are not the sex fiends or savages white people say they are, that they go overboard to leave the natural activity of sex out of their work. Freedom to write what one wishes to write has never been a fully realized concept, particularly for black authors. One example will do: while Chester Himes' so-called sex novel, *Pinktoes,* works beautifully as satire, in the area of sex it is, even for its time, pretty timid. Aside from James Baldwin's *Another Country,* Cecil Brown's *The Life and Loves of Mr. Jiveass Nigger,* perhaps my own novel, *All-Night Visitors,* and one or two others, the coast is clear. Novels that deal openly with sex as a part of the natural sequence of human experience are clearly free from the bad influences of modern Christianity. Not many American writers, black or white, can claim such freedom.

2. The Critic

From the early 1960s to 1971 the tension and conflict and change among and between black and white critics over the function of black writing spread a print and verbal façade that consistently conceded many other valid questions. In his introduction to *The Black Aesthetic* Addison Gayle, Jr., tells us he does not expect the contributors to his anthology to agree with him. "These are independent artists who demand the right to think for themselves . . ."[6]

I will now add to the chaos by injecting my own theory—

not a new one. My own feeling is simple: the most functional and valid method of examining a work of art is by first discovering the terms on which it exists and then judging it on its own terms alone. The racial identity of a group of writers is not grounds for a critical formula to which all may be subjected for analysis. Furthermore artistic values, red, blue, white, green, black or gold, do not have to give way to sociopolitical concerns. These concerns are not the sole function of art. Art gives vision to life and its traditions are for reference and roots. It is to be improvised on and extended, if not broken.

In the introduction to *The New Black Poetry* I speak of a "radical black aesthetic."[7] I am not referring there to some sort of jive, rigid formula. I mean a *new* attitude of freedom of expression, a new approach, from within, to one's experience, *being*. A new way of understanding the interplay between one's conscious and unconscious life—how this activity moves through the world. A new vision of art produced by black people—to move the new set of eyes out into the open. I do not mean "black aesthetic" as an extension of Black Nationalism. I feel the need to make this clear because it *is* what most black critics mean when they use the term.

The Black Critic. Black critics are busting out everywhere, asserting a new image. But the *effects* left by the image are not new. For example Harold Cruse, like many other black critics, spends a great deal of time attacking many black poets and novelists and playwrights. Something good, after all, may come out of feuds. Feuds may also be contained in one critic. As an example, Imamu Amiri Baraka's ideas seem to change very rapidly, and it is helpful that he dates his critical pieces as he goes along. In an issue of the *Journal of Black Poetry* Joe Goncalves, its editor, attacks poet Bob Kaufman and novelist Ishmael Reed. Goncalves dismisses Kaufman as "programed to lose" and concludes that Reed is, among other things unkind, "dependent" and laying dead at "the white man's fort."[8] Reed's rebuttal states, "The young people of this country desperately need a critical journal of vigorous and excellent standards, not a black variation of *Confidential* or *Key-hole* . . ."[9] Albert Murray, too, takes careful but disguised shots at quite a few of his own contemporaries. Julius Lester, however, attacks in a more open manner many excellent writers like Cecil Brown. In contrast, Larry Neal, in the December 1970 issue of *Black World,* shows a refreshing shift from his old outlook of Cultural Nationalism in his somewhat positive essay on Ralph Ellison. Meanwhile, Don L. Lee arrives on the scene. He tells white critics to mind *their own* business. But I like best critics like Sherley Anne Williams who concern themselves primarily with *the work.* The old timers, who mostly fill up Addison Gayle, Jr.'s, *The Black Aesthetic,* as far as I know still go around, like Nick Aaron Ford, encouraging all black writers to write "social propaganda," while people like Hoyt W. Fuller and John Henrik Clarke seem to work overtime in the interest of a very traditional idea: advancing Cultural Nationalism.

The White Critic. We all know of the Irving Howe-Ralph Ellison debate and its outcome, but few may realize that white Howe continues his hassle with black writers. In an article in *Harper's* he writes of Ishmael Reed: "He may intend his books as a black variation of Jonathan Swift."[10] In a letter to the same magazine Reed expresses his reaction. He correctly accuses Howe of lumping "together in a cultural slave quarters" black writers "of diverse aesthetics." Reed continues: "Howe writes of my novels in typical White chauvinistic manner . . . under the guise of criticism." Howe performs police work for a dying culture. "A dying culture will always call up its intellectual warhorses—no matter how senile they may be—"[11]

Irving Howe is far from the only white critic who, when viewing works by black writers, appears to be either silly or uncertain or both. Richard Gilman, a white critic with a hands-off attitude when it comes to black writing, imagines he is helping black critics and writers by withholding his opinions of their works. He expresses this feeling in a long essay called "White Standards and Negro Writing."[12] For what it is worth, Robert Bone, in his book *The Negro Novel in America,* seems to have his slow painful heart in the right place in that he attmepts to examine black fiction *as* art; but because he does so on European-American standards, most black critics would not give him the time of day, let alone a good word. Then there is Kenneth Rexroth, who, when he knows what he is talking about, appears to be fair in his judgment. But John O'Brien, Abraham Chapman, Jerome Klinkowitz and C.W.E. Bigsby obviously are better informed on black writing.

One final example of an ultimately silly white critic is Edward Margolies, who characterizes the poems in the anthology, *The New Black Poetry,* as "proletarian."[13] This amounts to calling John A. Williams, Al Young, Herbert A. Simmons, Larry Neal, June Jordan, Bob Kaufman, LeRoi Jones, Calvin C. Hernton, David Henderson, Nikki Giovanni, and Ed Bullins, second-rate authors. But Kenneth Rexroth says the same book is by far the broadest and best balanced and least sectarian of any of the new collections."[14] At the same time a white publication in Canada writes that the poems are too "subjective" and "reactionary."[15] So one can see there is diversity among white critics.

3. Special Problems

Finally, when considering the economic situation of black writers, so many other related problems begin to emerge, and I remember Langston Hughes' words: "The Negro writer in America has all the problems any other writer has, plus a few more."[16] As a member of an economically and socially oppressed group the black novelist does not move through the world in the same way Norman Mailer might. Despite the fact that there is not a lot of evidence that black writers receive smaller advances on their books than do white writers, to listen to a group of black novelists informally discussing their problems, not only would this seem to be true, but one also would come away feeling that too many white publishers un-

.destand too little about the black books they publish and, what is worse, care even less.

What about black publishers, then? In this oversimplified world of black and white, the black publisher is in a bind. Of the handful of black book publishers in the United States it seems only John H. Johnson is relatively free of both economic and trade problems. The others on the current scene, Broadside Press, Third Press, Drum and Spear, Third World Press, Julian Richardson, and Emerson Hall, all seem to share a common set of misfortunes: a lack of money and of trade support. One black publisher, Alfred E. Prettyman, President of Emerson Hall, put it in this way: "At best the business is a difficult one in which to stay afloat. For investors the payoff can only be over the long haul. Our problem is that too many quarters, whether from good intentions or ill, would keep us out."[17]

Obviously at best this has been a quick and short look at a very large area of work and activity. In concusion I would say the writer who "owns" his own mind stands the best chance of doing real, solid work. And the critic who wishes to see with a clear eye is the one who dismantles the self as much as possible of old notions about what black writing should or should not be. Such a person does not oversimplify such matters—or any matters—strictly along racial lines.

The special problems of the black writer, on the other hand, are rooted in the social, economic, political, historical and racial troubles of the United States and the entire white world; and, as we know, they will not be resolved, or even cleared away for more and different problems, without revolutionary change throughout this society and in the sensibility of people everywhere.

Notes

1 "A Black Criterion," *Journal of Black Poetry*, Spring, 1967.
2 "Theme and Structure In Boles' *Curling*: An Interview with The Author," *Black Academy Review*, Vol. 1, No. 1, 1970.
3 Quoted in "The Black American Writer" by C.W.E. Bigsby, *The Black American Writer*, ed. by C.W.E. Bigsby, Everett/Edwards, Inc. 1969.
4 "Indivisible Man" by Ralph Ellison and James Alan McPherson, *The Atlantic*, December, 1970.
5 Quoted in *The Negro Novel in America*, 1965 Revised Edition, by Robert A. Bone.
6 *The Black Aesthetic*, ed. by Addison Gayle, Jr. Doubleday & Co., Inc., 1971.
7 *The New Black Poetry*, ed. by Clarence Major; International Publishers, 1969.
8 *Journal of Black Poetry*, Vol. 1, No. 2, 1969.
9 Quoted from an Open Letter to Joe Goncalves by Ishmael Reed, dated, January 20, 1970.
10 "New Black Writers" by Irving Howe, *Harper's*, December. 1969.
11 *Harper's*, March, 1970.
12 "White Standards and Negro Writing" by Richard Gilman, *The New Republic*, reprinted in *The Black American Writer*, 1969.
13 *Library Journal*, June 1, 1969.
14 *The New Black Poetry*, ed. by Clarence Major, International Publishers, 1969; back cover of 4th printing.
15 *Literature & Ideology*, No. 2, Summer, 1969.
16 "The Bread and Butter Side", by Langston Hughes, *Saturday Review*, 1963.
17 *Publisher's Weekly*, March 25, 1971.

The Explosion
Of Black Poetry

Poetry is history and music and the organic stuff of your mind; poetry is the way you think and live and see and hear; poetry is all the shapes of yourself; it is sound and it is print; it is speech and craft; and a poem when it truly works is the language of your profoundest experience; it is your eye and voice in the world. But what is black poetry?

We know we are experiencing a great black cultural revolution and at the forefront of this healthy explosion is black poetry.

In 1968, when I wrote the introduction to *The New Black Poetry,* I observed that most other anthologies of "American poetry have been compiled either along lineal or historical lines." But I went on to say that "my own anthology, which contained the work of 76 contributors, was more cultural than racial." I pointed out that, "at least again as many (76), equally gifted Afro-American poets active today, might have been selected."[1] Well now I would say at least twice that combined number of new black poets are in circulation. The main and most important impetus for this fact is the Black Consciousness which has grown out of the racial and social struggle of the 1960s.

The works by most of these new poets are mainly confined to publications with limited outlets, such as various black student organs and mimeographed booklets. Others find outlets through music recording companies, on records and tapes. Still others communicate their poetry mainly by way of public

33

readings. With the same sort of energy generated by black students engaged in poetic expression, black poetry is also pouring out of prisons. Ironically, it is there that, for the first time, many black men and women have the brutal but necessary time during confinement in which to express themselves in writing, to discover new areas of themselves, to reach back to and carry on the personal and social themes of black ancestry.

The roots and sources of today's black poetry are steeped in the black folk and oral tradition. This tradition encompasses all those fantastic tall-tales and jokes our grandparents used to tell us; the themes of black gospel preaching, the spirituals and work songs, the blues—both country and city—all make up this lively, beautiful tradition. Darwin Turner, in the introduction to Zora Neale Hurston's book of Negro folktales and voodoo, *Mules and Men,* says, "Black folks in Florida tell about . . . a man so fast that he could walk seven or eight miles into the woods, shoot at a deer, run home, put his gun away, run back to the woods, chase the deer, and hold it until the bullet hit . . ." This is the sort of myth that helped to sustain the courage and faith of Black people and at the same time to lay the foundation for today's black poetry. "A myth," as defined by anthropologist Levi-Strauss, "is a story that aims to explain why things are as they are."[2] That rich folk-tradition drew on almost every aspect of life you can imagine, such as master and slave relations, fights, swimming, stealing, eating, sleeping, dreaming, and a wide variety of animals, especially the rabbit, the bear, the hawk, the buzzard, and the chicken; but more particularly it had its source in the awesome nature of the unknown and gave our ancestors the scare tales and the Lord and Devil tales as well as the mood for the spirituals.

Like the oral material of the folk experience, the early black literary poetry continued the effort to express and sustain black hearts, despite the European-American literary influence.

The folk tradition was nearly lost, however, during the last years of the nineteenth century, in the hands of black literary poets (such as Frances E.W. Harper). Anyway, with the

1920s, the spirit of the folk tradition was revived and flourished in the works of such poets as Jean Toomer and Langston Hughes.

The 1920s was also the period when Langston Hughes wrote and published a very important essay, "The Negro Artist and the Racial Mountain." In it he said, "An artist must be free to choose what he does . . . but he must also never be afraid to do what he might choose." Hughes went on to say that the new black writers (1926) were going to express themselves "without fear or shame. If white people are pleased, we are glad. If they are not, it doesn't matter. We know we are beautiful. And ugly too . . . If colored people are pleased, we are glad. If they are not, their displeasure doesn't matter either."[3]

This simple and healthy attitude has always been the premise of the strongest work by black poets and writers. To be a person reflecting one's deepest individuality as well as the culture that produces one is the truest function of the artist. While the Harlem Renaissance writers were rebelling against the whole nineteenth century way of thinking—the European Romantic tradition, with its formulas and melodramas—they were, at the same time, not only rediscovering the roots of black culture but extending them as well and laying the foundation for the spirit of black writing today.

Though many were independent thinkers, a number of the black poets writing during the last part of the nineteenth and the early part of the present century were given to viewing the world through one ideology or another—in both political and cultural terms. Some advocated nationalism, others pushed for integration. Still others found religious "solutions" to the problems of black people. During the earlier periods, poets such as George Moses Horton, Frances E.W. Harper, Albert A. Whitman, James Edwin Campbell, W.S. Braithwaite, Leslie Pinckney Hill, Georgia Douglas Johnson and Angelina W. Grimke were among the most widely published; around and after the turn of the century, we encountered the works of Paul Lawrence Dunbar, James Weldon Johnson, Claude McKay,

Jean Toomer, Countee Cullen, Langston Hughes, and later Owen Dodson, Melvin B. Tolson, Frank Horne and Robert Hayden.

The most common themes in black poetry (and in black fiction, too) have been universal ones—love, hate, sex, violence, death, the search for identity—and they have almost invariably involved the rebel hero (both male and female) and that other infamous hero, the black trickster, who lives by his wits, surviving in a hostile oppressive white society. Within the framework of their experiences, many black poets have dealt extensively with the images and heroes of black music, illuminating the lives and beauty of various great musical geniuses. Other topics frequent in black poetry are riot scenes, the black man-white woman syndrome, the idea of soul, the spirit of the suffering artist, the cityscape, impressions and implications of Africa as a motherland, program-ideas for changing the social and political policies of the United States, the problems of black students, situations unique to the black family, migration from country to city, spiritual testimonies to Blackness, parent and child relations, young love, the art of Coolness, the Vietnam war and other wars from a black perspective, the brutal United States legal system, and the cold, distant ways of many white folks. These topics, subjects, and themes are, when handled well, understandable anywhere by anyone, because when they are dealt with in terms of art, coming from a deep human level, the works themselves transcend the social structure and psychological pressures that produced them.

The original word, the spoken word, is closer to the black cultural tradition than the printed word. All people, of course, come from the spoken-word way of life but in this society black people are still culturally closer to it than whites. I recently expressed in this way: "Our language is born of sound clusters as opposed to Shakespeare's, which derives from the nexus, sight." So it is no surprise that, on the reading circuit, most black poets not only are more at home but also receive a better response, particularly from black audiences. That black people tend to be more ear-oriented than eye-oriented in cultural matters is another indication of our closer link with all that is considered "natural" as opposed to technological. Unfortunately, however, this is probably also the main cause of the fact that so many Black Power poets publish poems that, on the printed page, not only *look* awful but are actually mediocre in every respect except possibly the oral.

The experience of *reading* poems in public is in a world separate from that of *writing* poems. To stand before an audience can be considered, to some degree, a performance. The poet becomes an entertainer. Witness the tremendous success of such groups as The Last Poets. They come along in a tradition that is rich and electric with energy. But they have more in common with Ray Charles and James Brown, with rock and roll and blues traditions, than with Paul Lawrence Dunbar and James Weldon Johnson, with the English language and Shakespeare. Naturally they turn to recording companies faster than or just as quickly as they do to book publishers. Broadside Press puts out a series of tapes of poets reading their own works, and a number of long playing records of black poetry readings have gone over very well: for instance, *The Last Poets* by The Last Poets, *On The Streets In Watts* by The Black Voices, *History Is Your Heartbeat* by Michael Harper, *New Jazz Poets, Tough Poems for Tough People.* (White poets record also, but print remains essentially where they are at.)

The audience for the new black poetry is both black and white. Although the black students in the nation make up the largest segment of this listening and reading audience, whites, self-consciously, also listen and read. Despite the fact that many young black persons are resentful of whites paying this much attention to what blacks are doing, whites will very likely continue to do so; although they are also likely, from now on, or for awhile, to keep to themselves their opinions of what they hear and see, for we have told them they are unqualified to judge what they hear or see of the Black Experience.

Since so few black poets are presented to the public through traditional white publishing channels, black poets generally are considered *different* (and they are!), outside the mainstream of European-American book and periodical industries. In recent years even fairly well-established black poets have depended on black-owned or black-oriented periodicals for the publication of their works. Such publications as *Black Creation,* the *Journal of Black Poetry, The Liberator, Black World (Negro Digest), Umbra, Cricket, Uhuru, Gumbo, Mojo, Black Expressions, Black Dialogue, Soulbook, Freedomways, A Time for Prophecy, Uprising, Loveletter, Coercion, Proud Black Images, Wakra, Focus In Black, Knombro, Black Culture Weekly, Nommo, Grassroots, Essence, Broadside* (series of broadsides), the *Broadside Annual, Black on Black, Afro-American Festival of the Arts, Black Ascensions,* etc., have served as vehicles for the printed works of the larger percentage of the new poets. At the same time, many of the more print-oriented poets also publish in a wide variety of white magazines and newspapers both in this country and abroad.

To compliment this expanding list of black literary and poetry magazines, black book publishing companies (and white companies with heavy black lists) are emerging, though understandably at a slower rate. On the present scene, we have Emerson Hall, Broadside Press, Julian Richardson, Third World Press, Third Press, Drum and Spear, and of course, the oldest and best-established, the John H. Johnson Publishing Company (which has made little or no effort to publish the creative works of black writers in book form).

An additional outlet for black poetry has been the anthology —the commercial anthology (text and trade) and that from the small press. The commercial books are published primarily by the white-owned companies. A torrent of black poetry anthologies has flooded the market place. Many of them have been gobbled up instantly by the black studies programs in schools across the nation. In 1968, *Black Voices, Dark Symphony, Potere Negro, Black Fire, I Am The Darker Brother, Ten: Anthology of Detroit Poets* and *Nine Black Poets* appeared, among others; in 1969 we saw *The New Black Poetry, City In All Directions, Black Arts, Cicory, Regroup, Black*

Poetry, From the Ashes, etc.; and 1970 brought *Natural Process, Poems by Black Poets, Today's Negro Voices, Soulscript, The Poetry of the Negro* and 3000 *Years of Black Poetry.* Numerous anthologies are of course already "available" from years before such as *An Anthology of Revolutionary Poetry, An Anthology of Verse by Negro Poets, Caroling Dusk: An Anthology of Verse by American Negroes,* all of which were published before 1930; and during the 1930's, *The Book of American Negro Poetry, American Stuff, Heralding Dawn: An Anthology of Verse,* appeared. During the bleak years of the 40s, the important *The Negro Caravan* and *Ebony Rhythm* were published. In the 50s came *Black and Unknown Bards* and the first edition of *The Poetry of the Negro.* In recent years, new titles have been *Ik Ben de Nieuwe Neger, American Negro Poetry, New Negro Poets, Sixes and Sevens, Beyond the Blues, Kaleidoscope, Black Expressions,* etc.. These are just a few of the trade books, to say nothing of volumes issued strictly as textbooks.

In Portnoy's Complaint Philip Roth was saying, in effect, what he had considered his Jewishness—until he went to Israel—was, in fact, nothing but a ghetto personality. Some of our new black critics are discovering that blackness (like Jewishness, or any other kind of racial or religious identity) can have many definitions. The best of our critics keep in mind the wide range of ideological perspectives from which black poets operate. It is not only the older black critics with their very fine white educations who are beginning to respect this fact but the younger hotheads as well. The older black critics still have a lot to teach us, even if only in the retrospective sense of supplying us with a sense of literary history—our own. For the newer critics such as Earl Ofari, Ron Welburn, Sharyn Jeanne Skeeter, Adam David Miller, and others, it is an asset to have the perspective which past criticism gives us on black poetry.

Nick Aaron Ford, Ernest Kaiser, Sterling A. Brown, Arna Bontemps, Alain Locke, and W.E.B. DuBois, each in his own way contributes as much to today's ultimate assesment of black poetry as do Hoyt W. Fuller, James A. Emanuel, Darwin T. Turner, Addison Gayle, Jr., Stephen E. Henderson, Richard Long, Johari Amini, Samuel Allen, Liz Gant, Calvin C. Hernton, Imamu Amiri Baraka, and other newer critics mentioned earlier. Of couse not *all* that is currently being contributed to the general body of black literary criticism is necessarily useful. Most of it is pretty worthless. But that is the way it is in any age among any people. What is important is the energy and excitement, the fuss. It is all very healthy and, once some perspective has been gained on what is actually being produced, on what is valuable and what is not, we can be sure that closer, more detailed judgments will be made.

The Black Academy of Arts and Letters, Inc., a new committee boasting a long list of impressive black leaders and artists, promises to fill the need of rewarding excellent work by black poets as well as other black artists. In 1971 the award committee was established and the works of many black poets were considered. Mari Evans' book, *I Am A Black Woman,* won the poetry prize. Elsewhere, awards and prizes have been set up in the names of Conrad Kent Rivers, Langston Hughes, Gwendolyn Brooks, and Imamu Amiri Baraka.

A few white establishments will occasionally acknowledge a black poet's work with an award, but this happens so infrequently that it is hardly worth mentioning. True, a number of black poets have received Guggenheim Fellowships or Whitney Opportunity Fellowships but white awards given to black poets are more likely to be for some sort of community arts projected. Yet in all fairness to some white institutions that give prizes to artists, it must be said that, since the end of the 1960s, a more "liberal" attitude toward black poets has been noticed. (Also, in discussing events and ideas in terms of black and white we would do well to remember that our world is never this simple but is reduced to this level for the sake of an argument.)

The contemporary black poets whose works I most enjoy are many and varied. I could not possibly deal with all of them in the space of this essay. Among the older poets, I especially like Robert Hayden and Gwendolyn Brooks. Those in my own age group whom I find particularly good are Calvin C. Hernton, Julia Fields, Ishmael Reed, Gerald William Barrax, Michael S. Harper, Jay Wright, June Jordan, Sam Cornish, Audre Lorde and Al Young. There are also several younger poets who I think are using their own voices well, such as Tom Weatherly and David Henderson.

Robert Hayden, by far one of the most skillful poets of his generation, has been widely neglected by both black and white readers and critics. Much of his work has appeared in white literary magazines with small circulation and his books have received almost no serious attention. He remains one of the few "major" American poets whose work has not been discovered. Referring to himself, Hayden once said: "Opposed to the chauvinistic and the doctrinaire, he sees no reason why a Negro poet should be limited to 'racial utterance' or to having his writing judged by standards different from those applied to the work of other poets."[4]

Gwendolyn Brooks, however, became a sort of big sister of the Black Power movement. Her name is often associated with the new Chicago movement in black poetry, headed mainly by Don L. Lee. "My obligation," Gwendolyn Brooks said a few years ago, "is to my poetry, to myself. The poetry is myself. When I sit down to write . . . it's because I've had an impression, an idea, an emotion."[5] Winner of white literary awards, her books had been published by a old, well-established white company since 1945. In recent years, however, she has turned to the black publisher, Dudley Randall, owner of Broadside Press. Her first book from this house is *Family Pictures* (1970). Yet for me her early work possesses an excellence rare in American poetry.

Of his own work, Calvin Hernton once wrote: "I write because I feel I am being outraged by life. I am *alone* and I am everybody . . . There is no 'reason' for the poetry I try to write; there is only cause . . ."[6] Though he has achieved international recognition as the author of *Sex and Racism in America,* Hernton is at his very best in poetry, which he enjoys writing. You can step on his brown suede shoes but don't step on poetry! His poems carry the power and drama of deeply felt and passionately thought-out emotions and concepts. And they are always hinged on concrete matter. He *shows* us rather than tells us.

Julia Fields, born in the south, has lived there most of her life, and as a girl she was soon "peddling vegetables, washing dishes, being a waitress and a telephone girl."[7] One of the best black women poets on the scene, she works quietly. Her work commands our respect; writers like Fields are the ones who are ultimately taken seriously. Now a high school teacher with a Bachelor's degree, she is one of the most intellectually crisp poets of her generation. Her images are always strong and sharp. She says, "In the future, the only relevant literature will be that which has gone directly to the heart of blackness."[8]

An example of one who goes directly to the heart of blackness is Ishmael Reed, who says, "I try to do what has never been done before."[9] He succeeds often. He gambles and wins a lot. One of the most original poets around, he is from Chattanooga but grew up in Buffalo, "where 'polack' is scribbled on the bust of Chopin in Humboldt Part."[10] He attended the University of Buffalo and later reflected that he himself "has been buffaloed by many aspects of American society."

Also from the south, Alabama, Gerald William Barrax in 1968 said of his work, "I can't make any profound statement on poetics because I never know what a poem is going to be . . . The poem is me as I write it. Anything else I might say about poetics would be a posture and a lie."[11] Speaking of Blackness and death, Barrax tells us, "They are implicit in all my responses to people and the world I live in and in everything I write,"[12] and we recognize his work to contain the distilled quality of our implicit experience as black people.

The same is true of Michael S. Harper. Of his first book of poems, *Dear John, Dear Coltrane,* Harper says: "What concerns me is the articulation of consciousness, the ability to deal with contingencies and create a new liberating vision which frees rather than imprisons."[13]

Equally serious in his struggle to bring from old words a new vision is Jay Wright. "Most of what I'm doing is "in progress' "[14] says Wright. From New Mexico, he is an ex-profesional football player, who in recent years has been "working on the idea that the grounds of myth, history and art are similar, if not the same . . . I'm trying to carry these investigations into perceptions and epistemology."[15]

June Jordan, not only a good poet but also a successful critic and teacher, has said of her own work, "Poetry is the way I think and the way I remember and the way I understand or the way I express my confusion, bitterness and love."[16]

One might easily say that "confusion, bitterness and love" are the qualities also found in Sam Cornish's poetry. A native of Maryland, during the 60s he was very active in the mimeographed-little-magazine revolution. Cornish feels that "some of the best modern poetry is to be found in the films of John Ford, Richard Lester and Samuel Peckinpaw . . ."[17] which may suggest the range of his concept of poetry.

An intense and brilliant poet whose work contains the singing quality of Dylan Thomas, Audre Lorde says of herself, "I am Black, Woman, and Poet—in fact and outside the realm of choice. I can choose only to be or not to be, and in various combinations of myself . . . The shortest statement of philosophy I have is my living, or the word 'I' "[18] She describes herself further as "a member of the human race hemmed in by stone and away from earth and sunlight."[19]

Not only sunlight, air and laughter, rain and tears, find their way into the work of Al Young, who spent his "shuttling childhood between southern & northern U.S."[20] and started "writing westerns, detectives & science fictions in notebooks around age ten."[21] The writing of poetry for him has its basis in a mystical experience he describes as "a vastness I feel growing within me that I could explore and delight in forever."[22] Poetry, he says, should expand us, give us "our quintessential selves."[23]

One poet who truly gives us himself—even if we do not always find ourselves in his work—is Tom Weatherly, the "holder of the double mojo hand &/ 13th degree gris-gris black belt." His poetry is intensely personal, made in a sort of shorthand. His codes, however, communicate black secrets—secrets we all know.

David Hendenson, "The Mayor of Harlem," a powerful, longwinded poet, is one of our very best. Of his book, *De Mayor of Harlem,* Henderson says: "I hope these poems go beyond the popular . . . joy to some mean point in there where you catch me bopping up and down the streets, dark and odd."

There are many other poets from the last three generations who deserve our attention. Undoubtedly, Sterling A. Brown, Margaret Walker, Ray Durem, Samuel Allen, Conrad Kent Rivers, Lennox Raphael, Imamu Amiri Baraka, Bob Kaufman, Stanley Crouch, N.H. Prichard, and too many others to list, are all strong voices. The newer poets of exceptional promise are Donald D. Govan, Charles F. Gordon, Sharyn Jeanne Skeeter, Quentin Hill, Quincy Troupe, Ron Welburn, Gayl Jones, Primus St. John, Joseph Major, Howard Jones, John Hall and Doughtry "Doc" Long. Though most of these writers do not yet have published books to their credit, their works appear in many of the publications mentioned earlier.

The black poet, like any other poet, needs recognition and encouragement. The sort of interest young black people are showing in the work of black poets is one of the most beautiful concerns to stay with us from the Black Consciousness boom of the 1960s. No longer (we hope) will the black poet have to suffer the ache of having his work critically evaluated mainly by a white audience. There certainly is nothing wrong with whites enjoying and even critizing black poetry. But one important thing for black poets and black people in general is: the white opinion will carry weight equal only to its value.

So I say crazy!

Notes

1 *The New Black Poetry,* International. 1969, pp. 19-19.
2 Levi-Strauss quoted in the *N.Y. Times Magazine,* 1972.

3 "The Negro Artist and the Racial Mountain", in *The Nation,* 1926.
4 *Kaleidoscope: Poems by American Negro Poets,* 1967.
5 *Conversations,* ed. Newquist, Rand-McNally, 1967.
6 *Sixes and Sevens,* Breman Ltd., 1962.
7 *Beyond the Blues,* Hand and Flower Press, p. 107.
8 *Negro Digest,* January, 1968.
9 *Dices or Black Bones,* Houghton Miflin Co., 1970.
10 *Yellow Back Radio Broke-Down,* 1969, (book jacket).
11 *The Young American Poets,* Follett, 1968.
12 *Another Kind Of Rain,* University of Pittsburgh Press, (book jacket), 1970.
13 *Natural Process,* p. 42, Hill & Wang, 1970.
14 Ibid.
15 Ibid.
16 *The New Black Poetry,* International, 1969.
17 *Natural Process,* Hill & Wang, 1970.
18 Ibid.
19 *Cables to rage,* Breman Ltd., 1970.
20 *Dices or Black Bones,* Houghton Miflin Co., 1970, p. 137.
21 *Natural Process,* op. cit. pp. 180-181.
22 Ibid.
23 Ibid.

Part Two

The Black Aesthetic

Edited by Addison Gayle, Jr.

There is not nor has there ever been any long-standing, healthy correlation between criticism and creativity. The notion of an "aesthetic" has the aroma of a sort of cultural dictatorship. (Personal criticism and personal creativity and personal aesthetics are another matter. I am referring to very public and very formal concepts.) However we can be thankful that there are no concrete standards or principles to which every black artist must adhere. The cultural fermentation current in the United States is radical, and that alone is the healthiest aspect of this new phase for Afro-American writers. The best black critics recognize this fact. This is not to say that the scene is not crowded with would-be dictators making frenzied efforts to squeeze every black person in the act of creating into the limitations of the network of one theory or another; some call it "The Black Aesthetic." Charles Wright does not produce books like those of Hal Bennett; and this, folks, is the real creative range and possibility we all can be proud of.

We are beginning to be confronted with a large number of new black critics. Unlike the older white-oriented critics, they have set for themselves the task of examining the work of black artists in what each, in his or her own way, calls black terms. It is a much better scene than what we had. I mean, it couldn't have been worse and we must trust that it will be better. However, brotherliness and sisterliness may not change the bad news between critics and creators.

Nevertheless there are many intellectual uses for criticism. Good criticism should *lead* the reader to the original work. The main thing to watch is that it might stifle creative work and eventually take its place and, in so doing, defeat its own function. Yet it is also the case that, in times when creative energy is low people usually turn to criticism. There is no excuse for such evasion now with so many new and good black writers around. Criticism we will read but we must sustain the will to turn directly to the works themselves.

The Black Aesthetic is a fairly good attempt to engage the question of black art. It is put together in five categories: Theory, Music, Poetry, Drama, and Fiction. It contains an introduction by the editor and 33 essays, mainly by older critics: W.E.B. DuBois and Alain Locke among others. The most interesting aspect of the book is the presentation of a number of new viewpoints, but the newer critics represented here are too few. Adam David Miller, Ron Welburn, and Ishmael Reed are new voices breaking different theoretical ground. However we need more and equally different ideas.

Personally, I would like to see many more books along this line to help replace the distorted criticism in that poverty-stricken corner reserved for blacks in the outhouse of white literary criticism.

Some Changes

Poems by June Jordan

Some Changes is June Jordan's third book, and before there was any book under her name, she had been widely published in periodicals, always showing sharp intelligence and keen observation, whether in a poem or an essay. Her first book, a juvenile, *Who Look At Me,* went over very big among adult readers. And her anthology, *Soulscript,* is the sort we've needed for our children for too many terrible years. These poems, *Some Changes,* hold you off and take you in at the same time. The energy from which they are generated is so overwhelming that each poem leaves the reader stronger for the reading thereof.

The introduction to the book, however, I found disconcerting. We should be able to assume that, *if* a book contains an introduction, it must need one. If it has one and doesn't need one, and if that fact is very obvious, then something is wrong. But when the wrong is blatant and even *forced* we may find it difficult to excuse. Julius Lester, poetry editor (!) for the publisher of the book, (whose main talent, as far as anybody can guess, lies in the area of political theory where, incidentally, he seems to do pretty well) has attached, sadly, to *Some Changes* a socio-political essay that is supposed to be about June Jordan and her poetry. For this reader, it did not seem to relate to either. June Jordan is not a Black Power poet, but Lester's approach to her work seems to begin from this assumption. I can't buy it.

51

Do not misunderstand. I have no argument with what the introduction says, in itself. My dissappointment is in its very presence in the book. Precious few people read poetry anyway and those few who might go seeking good poetry could easily be turned off by the implication of such an introduction, assuming that June Jordan is just another loudmouth dialect poet. I say this to encourage the lovers of interesting poetry to check out *Some Changes* despite its lead piece. June Jordan gives a beautiful, black performance of the soul as she takes us through her changes.

cathechism
of d neoamerican
hoodoo church

Poems by Ishmael Reed

Ishmael Reed, the carrier of the Hoodoo Bird, is an "astro-soul detective," a necromancer whose poems and novels cast spells on the empty, die-hard-Euro-American Literary Establishment. On the dustjacket of his anthology, *19 Necromancers From Now,* he says: "Dance and Drums preceded the word. Thousands of years before the invention of the novel or the short story, Thoth, the black Birdman of Egypt, 'invented letters' and 'gave names to things.' " And again: "Some plant their flags on things; we plant our flags on the seventies."* He means it and is in the process of proving it with each new book he does.

In this collection of his own poems, *catechism of d neoamerican hoodoo church,* as in all his work, Reed shows an intense awareness and makes use of his historical and cultural background, tracing it to the East rather than the West. This is Reed's first book of poems and it contains some of his finest to date. The strongest aspect of this collection is Reed's original style and his use of carefully researched historical and religious material. His originality is intense and as captivating as his

---

* *19 Necromancers From Now,* ed. by Ishmael Reed, Doubleday & Co. Inc., 1970.

humor, a quality modern poetry has long needed. The poem "I am a cowboy in the boat of Ra", which first appeared in my own anthology, *The New Black Poetry,* I consider one of the best poems in contemporary American literature. Another important poem is "Badman of the guest professor," dedicated to several black artists and also to "d mysterious 'H' who cut up d rembrandt."

Reed leaves some curses "in d cash/box" and speaks to the man on his way out: "listen man, i cant help it if yr thing is over, kaput,/finis . . ." Which is clear enough.

Blueschild Baby

A Novel by George Cain

George Cain's novel, *Blueschild Baby* is the story of a young black named Cain who attempts to come to terms with his own situation as a victim of both racism and hard-core drugs. It expresses a wide range of conflicting emotions, past and present. In the end the hero, a drifter just out of prison, leaves his white sweetheart because she is white and takes up with a black girl, not, it seems, because he loves or even sees her as a lovable person but because she is black, and also, perhaps, because Black Consciousness is In. Regardless of how he sees his black woman, she does help him kick his drug habit and they live happily ever after—wc hope.

Novels about the drug scene are done to death, but if one comes along that deserves some serious attention we should give it notice. The most impressive aspect of this work, for this reader, is the very promising quality of the writing itself. The book also demands our consideration because it is written in the context of social realism. Traditionally, social realism has been the black writer's mode of expression. Ralph Ellison and several other broke the pattern, and today, many new black novelists push beyond these old structural and theoretical limitations.

The deep agony of one hooked on physically addictive drugs (because of the hassle involved in getting the stuff), together with its social implications in a racist society, is a subject which the "surface" storytelling approach of social realism cannot embrace successfully. In fact that approach cannot do justice to any aspect of today's reality because it obviously does not deal with the whole experience, internal and external, and the interplay between the two. We get very small flashes of it in Cain's book but the final effect is that we feel tricked.

A writer's angle, however, *is* himself and the way he has to be—at least at the moment of his writing. This reader is happy to have found indications in this first novel that George Cain might actually burst out of the confines of his method of using social realism. No one wants to feel cheated by the author of any novel. Happily, Cain's language and form seem to be straining to do more than they are allowed to do in this work.

Black authors, like white ones, who have handled the drug scene well are few. For example, Clarence L. Cooper, Jr. in his novel, *The Scene* (1960), and again in *The Farm* (1967), really shows us not only the junkie's plight but also the system that controls his life. Yet he fails to get to the level of "inner experience" and how it relates to external action. Meaning has to be dramatized, not explained. Of course the reader wants to be shown, not told, but in showing, the author is also expected to give to the experience described a sense of wholeness. William Burrough's *Junkie* also fails the inner experience, his *Naked Luch* neglects the external; his son's book, *Speed,* which reads like a journal, is, just as Allen Ginsberg describes it, "dead-pan," and gives no real sense of what it is like to be strungout on methedrine. Cain, despite his occasional tendency to preach *at* you, does carry you along inside the narrator's mind, which, by the way, may be part of the problem. The way the author does it, however, satisfies those looking for fictional journalism.

In the end, however, Cain manages to leave the impression of having been honest and even a little passionate. But *Blueschild Baby* obviously comes nowhere near being the best novel of the black experience since Richard Wright's *Native Son,* as one black critic in *The New York Times* claimed it to be. We can hope, though, with George Cain, as his narrator says, that he will "someday . . . emerge as George Cain." He may make it both as a person and as a writer.

The Autobiography
Of Miss Jane Pittman

A Novel by Ernest J. Gaines

Ann Petry, in her masterpiece, *The Narrows,* showed us the plight of a black man through the sort of rare skill and power few writers have managed. Now, Ernest J. Gaines, in *The Autobiography of Miss Jane Pittman,* presents us whith a fictional portrait of a black woman, the quality and range of which no woman writer, to my knowledge, has given us in print. Perhaps we might then say that the perspective one sex has on the other becomes an essential key to a larger vision of the other.

Whether or not you accept this theory, Gaines' novel achieves a level of strength and a tone, steeped in historical experience, that is as impressive as the stoical endurance and courage of his heroine Miss Jane. Also, Gaines' method avoids the obvious pitfalls of social propaganda, by a relentless use of black folklore along with and throughout Miss Jane's narrative as well as the imposition of ideological concepts upon us or upon his story. However, he never permits us to forget the oppresive social and political framework in which black people, as seen through Miss Jane's eyes, move and struggle. The result is a very controlled, artful story; equally important, its drama—dialogue and narration— are delivered through its syntax, rather than through the cheap tricks of written dialect that too often plague our fictionists and poets.

Miss Jane's story begins in 1864, at the end of the Civil War, in Louisiana; she is a small but strong girl, impressed by the soldiers from the North. One in particular, Corporal Brown, becomes a symbol of freedom for her and, since he is from Ohio, Jane, now free along with all the other ex-slaves in the South, decides to take advantage of this unclear "thing" called emancipation and innocently sets out, to walk to Ohio and a larger sense of freedom. Though she never succeeds in leaving the state of Louisiana, her story, and the hundred and nine years of her life, become a prism through which our consciousness and spiritual lives, the quality and range of our mores, are affirmed and renewed.

Through it all, Miss Jane survives a devoted common law husband, Joe, and two spiritual sons, Ned and Jimmy. These three men in Jane's life are killed, each in his separate attempt to be a man of dignity. With a deep religious sense and mystical perception, Miss Jane's vision of the world and human activity leaves us feeling the true heartbeat of the winter and fall, spring and summer of our ancestors. We feel their pride and greatness, determination and honesty, tenderness and sorrow, humor and warmth. We come away knowing not only real black men, women and children, but also a number of white people who are not merely oversimplified as bad or good symbols or stereotypes—a short coming which, unfortunately, occurs often in fiction and poetry attempting a sociopolitical theme of this magnitude.

Whether or not one chooses to believe that a novelist should try to solve social problems through his work, there simply is no evidence that social propaganda has ever helped anybody toward a larger or deeper vision and sense of life. On the other hand, real art, such as this book represents, does achieve this goal. Real works of art stand up and prove themselves over and over. We may be sure and pleased to remember that an artist such as Ernest J. Gaines is, in the most important, though perhaps not the most accessible sense, our true revolutionary.

Part Three

Richard Wright:
The Long Hallucination

The story of Richard Wright's career, perhaps more than that of any other black American writer, not only illustrates the high and low points such an author can reach, in terms of his work and how it is received, but also dramatizes sharply the general problems of an independent career in writing. I will examine here the activities of Wright's writing career, some aspects of his personal life, the actual works he produced, and touch on correlations among these aspects in the hope of achieving not only a better understanding of his life as a writer but also with the suggestion of what such a life means for a black writer in a culture that is largely white.

When the novel *Native Son* was published in 1940, it sold out in all the bookstores in Manhattan within three hours. It became an overnight bestseller. The author, Richard Wright, became one of the prominent figures in American literature.

Who was he and what was he really like? "His voice was light and even rather sweet," James Baldwin says in *Nobody Knows My Name*. Most of the bare facts are well known. In *Black Boy*, one of the greatest autobiographies ever written, Wright told the tragic story of his childhood in the South. When he was born in Mississippi on September 4, 1908, his mother Ella was determined that her son would not grow up to become just another dirt farmer like his father, Nathaniel Wright. It seems reasonably safe to assume though, that she never once dreamed that he would ever become the world famous figure he became, particularly since her initial reaction to his first published short story, "The Voodoo of Hell's Half-Acre," was negative.

I often wondered about that story. Of it he writes in *Black Boy*: "It resolved itself into a plot about a villain who wanted a widow's home . . . . It was crudely atmospheric, emotional, intuitively psychological, and stemmed from pure feeling." This does not sound like a very bad premise for writing fiction, though apparently Wright later thought so.

The story, his first, was published in the *Southern Register*, the local Negro newspaper in a town where Richard, his brother Alan and his mother Ella, now separated from her husband, were living with Richard's grandmother, Margaret Wilson. Margaret Wilson was a very religious and superstitious woman. Hearing of the story she called Richard and asked him if it were a true story. It was not, he told her. Then it was a lie, she said. As a lie, Grandmama Wilson continued, it was surely the work of the Devil! The Devil had certainly got into Richard! Ella, his mother, took it to be a sign of a lack of seriousness. She worried about her son. She told Richard, "You won't be able to get a job if you let people think that you're weak-minded."

Wright met opposition to his early efforts not only within his family but outside as well. One day he was doing an odd job for a white woman in her home when she asked him what he wanted to become when he grew up. A writer, he told her. The woman was shocked and warned him that no colored boy could ever become a writer. She told him to set his heart on something more practical.

Referring to this time in his life he wrote, " . . . In me was shaping a yearning for a kind of consciousness, a mode of being that the way of life about me had said could not be, must not be, and upon which the penalty of death had been placed . . . ." So in a sense his will to change was the root of his hope and survival. He would run away to the North. He would try to come to terms with his own heritage, understand its implications and find a means to a better life.

Wright arrived in Chicago on a freezing day in December,

1927. The city seemed unreal to him and he was soon disappointed. But he would not go back.

While living with his Aunt Maggie, one of his mother's sisters, he worked in a delicatessen and later at the post office. Before long his mother and brother joined them. During these days he began the long and painful struggle to teach himself to write. He turned out many crude stories and poems and, on the side, read everything he could get his hands on. A self-conscious Negro boy with a southern accent, he had no social life—he couldn't even dance.

One year passed into another but time did not kill Wright's desire to master his chosen craft and art. In the most wretched kind of poverty, no longer working at the post office, he took a job sweeping the streets and continued to read and write after work into the wee hours. Eventually the family went on welfare and through the caseworker, Mary Wirth, Wright got his first break. In addition to finding a better job for him, she persuaded her husband, Dr. Wirth, a well-known sociologist at the University of Chicago, to give the young, beginning writer a list of books to read. Naturally, he read them all and was hungry for more. Meanwhile, also thanks to Mary Wirth, Wright became publicity agent for the local Federal Theatre Project, a government-sponsored cultural project to help with the theatrical unemployment problem during the Depression. While the people in the theatre group wanted to see staged plays showing the "sweet" side of black life, Wright argued with them; he felt that the bitter hardship of black life should be presented on stage. Throughout the work he would do later this attitude would be obvious.

When Mary Wirth was promoted to chief social worker of the Seventh Chicago Works Progress Administration, she secured for Wright a job as a professional writer in another WPA program. He became manager of essays for the Illinois Writers' Project. Meanwhile he was listening to the political speeches being made in Washington Park, and he soon started attending Communist meetings at the John Reed Club. It seemed to him that, at last, he had found a means of revolutionary expression in which the Negro experience could find new value and a new role. Very soon his poems began to appear in various magazines that supported Communist ideas, and in 1932 he officially joined the John Reed Club. He met people here who later became characters in his books. Eventually he became the club's "executive secretary."

Always a very serious and honest man, Richard Wright believed that this social philosophy would make a new and better life possible for *his* people, black people. He now wanted to show in his stories how Communism could relieve black suffering.

Accepting the position of Harlem Editor of *The Daily Worker*, Wright moved to New York in the Spring of 1937 at the age of 29. He liked New York but still felt closer to Chicago and continued to write about his experiences there and in the South. In his new job he met many new people. One of them was a 19-year-old boy from Oklahoma named Ralph Ellison, who had come to see Wright because he had read some of Wright's poems and liked them. In school Ellison had majored in music but was also interested in writing. Fifteen years later he would become established as one of the United States' outstanding writers when his book, *Invisible Man*, won the National Book Award.

During this time Wright assembled a collection of his stories and entered it in a contest sponsored by the Federal Writers' Project. Nobel Prize author Sinclair Lewis was one of the judges. Wright's work won the top prize of $500. Before long Wright's earnings from his work were enough to support him. *Uncle Tom's Children*, the prize-winning collection of stories, was published in a special edition by the Federal Writers Project. Even better, Harper & Brothers offered Wright a contract to publish the book for the general public; the author would receive 15½ percent of the wholesale price of each copy sold and $1300 as an advance on expected royalties. Wright accepted.

Meanwhile Wright was working on *Native Son* while living in one room in the apartment of a friend in Bedford-Stuyvesant, Brooklyn. At about this time he met the ballet dancer, Dhima Meadman, who later became his first wife; it was also at this time that he met Ellen Poplar, a social worker, who even later would become his second and final wife.

Uncle Tom's Children had made Wright famous. It was a bestseller and he was making more money than ever before in his life. He was also working harder than ever trying to finish *Native Son*. When the book was published in 1940 by Harper, it was an overnight smash success and Wright's name was inserted on the "Wall of Fame" at the New York World's Fair that year. More money than he had dreamed possible swelled his bank account. *Native Son* was a Book-of-the-Month Club selection, bought for $9,380. Yet Richard Wright remained calm. Already he was quietly working on a new novel.

With Paul Green, Wright wrote a dramatic version of *Native Son*. It appeared now on Broadway, starring Canada Lee as Bigger Thomas. Bigger is seen as a "bad nigger". In the play, as in the novel, he kills a white girl accidentally and out of fear; then to hide his deed he stuffs the body into a furnace. Obviously from this point there is no way for Bigger to turn back. But he feels suddenly alive for the first time in his life. The crime liberates him (whereas in a white novel, *Sister Carrie* by Theodore Dreiser, the hero's crime ultimately leads him to destruction, inwardly as well as outwardly).When Bigger tells his colored girl friend what he has done, she becomes afraid of him, so he kills her too and begins his flight from the police. He is captured and brought to trial, defended by a Communist lawyer; but Bigger is no longer just the shadow of a person. He *is* somebody! He *feels* important, He is *seen*. People look directly *at* him. Bigger goes proudly to the electric chair to die at the hands of a society that condemned him from birth.

1941 was also the year that Wright's book *12 Million Black Voices: A Folk History of the Negro in the United States* was published. It is a long poetic essay illustrated with photographs, which deals with black life in both the South and the North.

Although Wright was having great success in his work, his

marriage was failing, and the novel which he was writing, "Little Sister," was also doomed to failure. It was rejected by Harper and remains unpublished, and this was a great disappointment to Wright.

After divorcing Dhima, Wright married Ellen Poplar in March 1941, and in April 1942 their first daughter, Julia, was born. Wright was a proud 33-year-old father.

Two years later he left the Communist Party which he had joined back in 1934. During recent years his relations with Party bosses had become strained. Many of them had strongly disliked *Native Son*. More important, Wright had come to believe that the Party meant to *use* Negroes for its own purposes. He had joined it in good faith and for a long time believed that they meant to make a new and better life for everybody. But then all his life Wright had had faith in some bigger and better ideas of life. In Mississippi his family was Seventh Day Adventist. He had been taught through that religion that earthly life wasn't a person's *actual* life, that the *real* life of a person came *after* death. It was a religion that few Negroes in the South followed and this fact had made Wright feel even more an outsider. The other boys and girls he knew were usually Baptists or Methodists. But Seventh Day Adventism was what he had been taught and it was what he believed as a child. It said, in effect, that *someday in the future* the suffering would stop and everything would be good for black people —for all people.

In a way, the Communist Party's plans for the future had made the same sort of promise to Wright. It was most painful to have to give up one dream after another.

Before Harper published Wright's famous autobiography, *Black Boy,* in 1945, his editor there asked Wright to cut the last third of the book, the chapters about his Chicago and New York experiences, saying the cutting was necessary because of the wartime paper shortage. But Wright didn't believe that was the reason; a great deal of the part that would have been cut dealt with aspects of Wright's activities as a Communist. Even before publication date *Black Boy* became a best seller. The sales figure was 30,000 copies. The success of the book, naturally, added considerable to Wright's fame in the United States and in other countries where it was in translation. Of course the reactions were not all favorable. An outraged senator from Mississippi rose up on the floor of the Senate and said the book was a "blasted lie." No bookseller in Mississippi would sell the book.

In the spring of 1946 the French government invited Richard Wright and his family to visit its country. The Wrights liked France and enjoyed their stay there. The following year they moved to Paris permanently. There, in January 1949, their second daughter Rachel was born.

In France Wright made many friends, many of them among the French writers known as existentialists. While the "rootlessness" of the existentialist philosophy was formally a European experience, Wright found it contained much meaning for him as a black man.

By 1953, Richard Wright had finished what is in the author's opinion, his best novel. He called it *The Outsider*. It concerns an intelligent black man, Cross Damon, who manages to switch identities with a dead man after a train wreck. The people he knew now think he is dead and Cross sees this as an ideal chance to escape his past and his troubles. Cross leaves Chicago for New York but troubles, rather than staying behind, follow and mount in intensity. In the end he realizes that he cannot escape who and what he really is.

The book was not a success. In the United States *The Outsider* had an advance sale of 13,500 copies, not very promising compared to his earlier sales. Richard Wright's popularity had waned since 1945. During this time the United States' wartime friendship with the Soviet Union had ended, and those who had belonged to the Communist Party were being branded by many as traitors. Senator Joseph McCarthy had started his witch-hunt for Communists and Communist sympathizers in the government, using the tactics of wild claims and unfounded charges. McCarthysm created fear of any connection with Communism, even of books written by Communists. And though Wright had quit the Party even before the end of the war, it was still well known that he had been a Party member. So, many American readers stayed away from his books and a large number of libraries even removed *Native Son* and *Black Boy* from their shelves in response to pressures from McCarthy's supporters.

In Europe, on the other hand, *The Outsider* sold quite well. In fact, some European critics considered it the most important novel to emerge from an American experience.

In *The Outsider,* Wright tried to probe beyond the social context of race into the "human condition," to put it one way, and in his next fictional effort, *Savage Holiday,* he gave up the category of race altogether. A gripping novel, *Savage Holiday* was rejected by Harper. Wright eventually sold it, however, to Avon, a paperback publisher, who gave him a $2,000 advance. As a paperback original it went by almost unnoticed in the United States, but in Europe, translated into German, Italian, Dutch, and French, the book sold quite well.

At this point Wright turned his attention to a kind of book new to himself. The first one was about West Africa's Gold Coast (now Ghana). He called it *Black Power: A Record of Reactions in a Land of Pathos.* It is the reflections, sharp and sensitive, of a black American on his first contact with Africa. It was published in 1954 by Harper but it sold poorly. By this time, Wright's bank account was very low, and he had to continue to work to earn a living. He obtained an advance of $3,000 from Harper to visit Spain and to write a book about its people and their lives.

To Richard Wright the Spanish seemed more primitive than the Africans. Though of African descent, in Africa Wright had found the African mind rather strange. He was forced to realize how much an American—or at least how little an African—he actually was. Richard Wright had difficulty relating to the African's emotions and thoughts. In Spain he felt a similar distance between himself and the Spanish. But he felt that Spain, unlike Africa, was not moving toward the future, was not a growing society.

While working on the book, which he called *Pagan Spain,* Wright continued to take deep stock of himself. Aware of many of his own prejudices, he worked to overcome them. He meant to see and write about Spain as honestly as he could. It was in *Pagan Spain* that Wright said: "I have no race except that which is forced on me. I have no country except that to which I'm obliged to belong. I have no traditions."

While working on the manuscript of *Pagan Spain,* Wright read in the newspapers about the world's first Asian-African conference, to be held in Indonesia. The idea excited Wright —he felt he had to attend. He put aside his unfinished book and flew to Djakarta. There he talked with local Asians as well as many of the delegates from other countries. He wrote about this experience in *The Color Curtain.* There, as in *Pagan Spain,* Wright's new vision of himself and the world continued to show itself, "Color," he wrote, "is not my country . . . I am opposed to all racial definitions."

The Color Curtain was rejected by Harper, and World Publishing Company published it in 1956, the year in which Harper brought out *Pagan Spain.* After this Wright finally broke all ties with Harper. He turned to Doubleday & Company, Inc. To them he submitted an outline of his novel, *The Long Dream,* and a contract with an advance of $6,000 was signed. At this time he also put together for Doubleday a thin volume of his essays and speeches, titled *White Man, Listen!,* which went by almost unnoticed by general readers. Meanwhile, neither *Pagan Spain* nor *The Color Curtain* was selling very well.

The Long Dream appeared in bookstores in 1958. It is the story of Fishbelly, a black boy growing up in Jackson, Mississippi. Not a "bad nigger" like Bigger Thomas nor an intellectual like Cross Damon, Fishbelly is middle class. His father, Tyree, an undertaker, is murdered by racist cops and local businessmen. To escape the fate of his father, Fishbelly flees to the North. He then heads for France. In this story Wright seems to be saying pretty much what he had previously said in his earliest short stories and in *Native Son*: to be black in the United States, particularly in the South, is a very fearful and tragic situation.

The actor Anthony Quinn was deeply moved by the book. He helped Wright with advice toward a stage production and Quinn himself, a white man, was anxious to play the role of Tyree. Three years later a good Broadway production of *The Long Dream* became a reality—but without Quinn. Cheryl Crawford, its producer, felt she couldn't afford the lowest salary Quinn would accept—$3,000 per week.

In spite of many discouragements, Wright did not give up. He still believed in himself and in what he had to say. All his life he had dreamed that things could get better. They *would* get better. Although his recent books had not done well, he finished a sequel to *The Long Dream* and called it *Island of Hallucination*. It tells of Fishbelly's adventures in Paris among Afro-American spies. The book was rejected by Doubleday, however, and this was one more great disappointment for Wright, who began to wonder if his writing career were over. Short of money, his daughters nearing college age, he considering teaching to make a living. He was not in the best of health, however. He was fifty years old now, and not nearly as strong physically as in the past. It exhausted him too greatly to work the long stretches he had managed previously.

Meanwhile, his oldest daughter entered Cambridge University in England, and his wife Ellen and the youngest daughter all took up residence in England. Richard Wright, for mysterious and unknown reasons, was denied the right to remain in England. Even close friends in the British government could not help him.

So in another apartment in Paris, on Rue Regis on the Left Bank, Wright brooded, staring out the window. He wrote hundreds of haiku poems, a form of poetry he had become fascinated by while in Indonesia. He was unhappy and he missed his family. Nevertheless he put together *Eight Men,* the first collection of his short stories since *Uncle Tom's Children.* However the book did not appear until after his death. Wright's health remained poor. He was being treated by Dr. Valadimir

Schwartzmann, an expert on tropical diseases, for what was at first thought to be an "amoebic infection." It was believed that he had picked up this infection while in Africa in 1953. But he never recovered, and information on the cause of his death is conflicting. Wright was abed in a clinic for a check up. It was near eleven o'clock when the nurse saw his signal. Just as she got to him, she saw him die—with a smile on his face.

I try to imagine the type of work Richard Wright would have done had he developed into another type of person. As a child he wrote a story that was of "pure feeling." In his latter work there was always some ideology behind everything. I like to play with the idea that that original innocence might have saved him from many hallucinations had he been able to save *it*.

James Baldwin:
A Fire in the Mind

James Baldwin has become what many people the world over consider the greatest American essayist since Ralph Waldo Emerson.

American public interest in Richard Wright had almost died out by 1950 and the white segment of the literary establishment had no really great "black star" with whom to replace him until James Baldwin published *Notes of A Native Son,* seven years later. Within seven more years Baldwin was to win recognition as an outstanding writer both at home and around the world.

The story of Baldwin's writing career, from its beginning to the last part of the 1960s, has wide meaning beyond itself when looked at along with aspects of his personal life and the actual work he produced.

Where does it begin?

From the moment James Baldwin learned to read he usually had a book in his hand. After he got a New York Public Library card, almost every day in the week he was going in and coming out of the 135th Street branch, always with an armful of books. In books he discovered people who suffered and loved, people who were afraid of things and people who were very brave. He began to see that the things he felt and thought about had also happened to others. It made him feel less alone in the world.

During World War II, Baldwin did not serve in the army, unlike many other boys in his neighborhood. He was given a draft-deferment because his absence would create hardship in the family. He wanted to become a writer, and he had been working hard toward this goal for many years. By the time he was 19 he had already written a great deal. Even before his father died around this time, Baldwin had begun to discover Greenwich Village. It was the part of the city where he felt most accepted—at first.

In the Village, Baldwin truly began to write. He held down one full-time job after another, but he spent his nights at his typewriter. He was so serious about what he was doing that he seldom got more than three of four hours' sleep at night. He was working on a novel which he called *In My Father's House,* a novel which was, in a way, an attempt to write *Go Tell It On The Mountain.*

Before long, unexpected luck came. He was introduced to the world-famous writer, Richard Wright. (Later, when Baldwin himself became famous and young writers started coming to him, he saw in them the same sort of fear he had had of Richard Wright.) As they talked, Wright told him that being a writer was always difficult; he also consented to take a look at the novel Baldwin was working on. Thinking it showed promise, Wright helped Baldwin to get a Eugene F. Saxon Memorial Trust Award.

This was his first real boost. Jimmy Baldwin almost dared think of himself as a "real" writer. Yet he knew he had to prove himself worthy of the grant and of Wright's faith in his work. Unfortunately Baldwin worked too hard on the book, and in so doing he somehow destroyed what was best in it. He had listened to the advice of too many well-meaning people. Publishers interested in it wanted him to rework it and give it a Richard Wright flavor, and friends offered their own opinions on how Baldwin should do his novel. Accordingly he kept on making changes, and in the end he had a hopeless manuscript.

The experience was very painful for Baldwin. How would he ever be able to face Wright again? Though he felt he had let the older writer down he knew he had failed himself even more. But he refused to quit. Rather, he quietly worked away days and hours and months at the typewriter, teaching himself to put words together in a way that might sincerely move or affect the people who read them. As he worked he came to realize that somehow he had to learn to become his own best critic, and to learn how to be a good rewriter.

One of Baldwin's first sales was that of a book review to *The Nation.* After that, *The New Leader* began to buy his articles. He was working nights as a waiter and spending all of his free time at his writing desk. It was very rough. Sometimes he felt he was about to crack up.

Baldwin was twenty-four when he met Robert Warshow, an editor on the staff of *Commentary,* the magazine of the American Jewish Committee. Warshow assigned him to do a piece on Harlem, and Baldwin worked extremely hard to make the piece good. Although Warshow had him rewrite parts of it, he never told Baldwin *how* to do it. The result was that Baldwin learned more on his own about his own writing problems, and the ways he found for solving them were sincerely his own. He was getting better all the time, and *The Partisan Review* began buying some of his articles.

Now Baldwin went to work on another novel, calling it *Ignorant Armies.* With a photographer named Theodore Pelatowski, he also put together a book about the storefront churches in Harlem. For it, Baldwin received a Rosenwald Fellowship. Though neither book was published, doing them provided valuable experience for Baldwin.

On a very personal level this was also a time of great self-consciousness and a period of confusion about which Baldwin himself has written a great deal in both his fiction and his nonfiction. He felt he had to leave New York, to leave the United States, to gain distance.

On November 11, 1948, Baldwin flew to France. With only $660 he had no idea how he would support himself, but he did not intend to come back.

In 1951 Baldwin was still trying to finish the novel that had been teasing his mind since he was nineteen years old. He was beginning to fear he would not be able to finish the book. Basically, he was working with the same subject matter he had handled in *In My Father's House*. In a friends' chalet high in the mountains of Switzerland he worked with a concentration that was not possible in Paris.

By late February, 1952, he had finished his novel, which he called *Go Tell It on the Mountain*. He and his friend walked down the mountain together to the post office to send the manuscript off to Helen Straus, the head of the literary department at the William Morris Agency.

Now Baldwin waited and hoped. Finally word came that Alfred A. Knopf, a very good publisher, liked his novel and there was a good chance that he would publish it. Just to make sure that chance was even better, Baldwin decided to go to New York to see the publisher. He took what money he had, and Marlon Brando, another friend of his, gave him enough so that he could buy a ticket. Baldwin landed in New York penniless, but this time he had prospects. In fact, after talking with the editor at Knopf, he was given a contract and an advance against royalties.

Quickly Baldwin returned to Paris and immediately started work on a second novel. Although the effort was a failure, he was able to use parts of it in a later novel, *Another Country*.

Thinking that it might have been a mistake to try another novel right away, Baldwin decided to try his hand at writing a play. *Go Tell It on the Mountain* was about black Americans and centered around a storefront church in Harlem. The play also was about storefront church life in Harlem. Baldwin called it *The Amen Corner*. . . .

Baldwin was still very poor, still very familiar with hunger and, because Paris was so expensive, he now chose to live in a small town near Chârtres, sharing expenses with three other poor artists. One rainy day in May he went into Paris to pick up his mail. Waiting for him at the American Express office were his ten free copies of *Go Tell It on the Mountain*. This was the first time he'd seen a book of his own in print, but on an empty stomach he could not possibly get excited about it.

In his need for a quiet place to write, Baldwin kept returning to the little chalet in the Swiss Alps. There he worked away, listening to a blues record by Bessie Smith. The weather was bitterly cold in the tiny mountain village. The people who lived there looked upon Baldwin as the funniest thing they had ever laid eyes on. Like innocent and curious children, they boldly felt his kinky hair and rubbed his skin to see if the color would come off.

Meanwhile in the United States, *Go Tell It on the Mountain,* while receiving good book reviews, was not selling any better than the average "first novel" of a new author. So for James Baldwin, promising novelist, poverty was still a huge reality —felt, among other places, intensely in the stomach.

In the south of France, James Baldwin finished (after some difficulty with the conclusion) a short novel he called *Giovanni's Room.* He considered it a fable about innocence—about how the loss of innocence can also *restore* innocence. Years later, he considered this his best novel (and, incidentally, this writer agrees with him). His earlier effort, *Ignorant Armies,* had been an attempt to say what he finally managed to say in *Giovanni's Room.*

Baldwin was increasingly lonely. The comfort he got from playing the spirituals and blues was not enough. He kept wondering what he was going to do with himself. Did he really want to spend the rest of his life in France? He would have to find out; so in 1955 he went back to New York to see how he felt about the United States.

By this time he had finished a great deal of work: a novel, a collection of essays, and a play. The play was to be staged by a college theatrical group at Howard University, and Baldwin went to Washington to watch them rehearse. Hearing it, seeing it, he could tell where the play went wrong, so he made many changes during the various stages of production. The experience taught him a lot about the requirements which a playwright must meet.

Meanwhile his publisher, Knopf, rejected *Giovanni's Room.* His editor felt that its sex theme would wreck Baldwin's career. His agent, Helen Straus, told him—according to Baldwin himself—that nobody was likely to accept such a book from him. Baldwin says her advice to him was, "Burn it." (However, Helen Straus denies giving such advice*.)

Instead of burning the manuscript, however, Baldwin went to England and sold it to Michael Joseph. Balwin's advance was only $400, and Joseph was doubtful about publishing such a book but he did. Baldwin's agent later sold the book to Dial Press, whose president had already expressed interest in adding Baldwin's name to his list of authors. The contract with Dial was for two novels and the advance was only $2000, and, though Baldwin was not happy with the deal, he signed the agreement anyway. He needed the money. He later remembered, bitterly, that his friend Norman Mailer received $125,000 from the same company.** Having made these arrangements, Baldwin returned to Paris and finished some revisions he wanted to make on *Giovanni's Room* before the American edition appeared.

Now was time to begin work on the really big novel. For the next five years he would be writing *Another Country*. At the same time Beacon Press, in Boston, bought and published his collection of essays, *Notes of a Native Son*. It became a bestseller. In the United States, Baldwin's name began to gain "weight." He was being talked about and even *read*. By word of mouth his fame as a writer steadily increased. Critics were saying he was one of the greatest writers of his generation. They had said *Go Tell It on the Mountain* showed promise. Now that promise was fulfilled.

Giovanni's Room came out in 1958. It did not climb to the top of the bestseller list, but Baldwin was happy with the reviews, and after awhile the novel even began to have a modest but steady sale. During the time he was working on his new novel he also took time out to put together another collection of essays, published by Dial rather than Beacon. The

---

* *The Furious Passage of James Baldwin* by Fern Marja Eckman, M. Evans, 1966, p. 137.

** *The Furious Passage of James Baldwin,* by Eckman, p. 138.

title, *Nobody Knows My Name,* seems to be a line from a Bessie Smith song—though Baldwin does not say this anywhere in the book. Already *Notes of a Native Son* had become an American classic. Now *Nobody Knows My Name,* subtitled "More Notes of a Native Son", hit all the nation's bestseller lists.

Baldwin was thirty-seven and could no longer think of himself as a young man. Although he regretted the passing of his youth, it was good to know that his dream of becoming a writer had come true. Now he wanted to keep going and get his work done.

The South had always been deep in Baldwin's mind. After all, the people of Harlem came mostly from the South. His own family and their life style had so much of the South about them that in many ways Baldwin felt as though he himself had been born in one of the southern states. Now, even before leaving Europe, he had his heart set on going down South where, at this very moment, policemen were beating and shooting black demonstrators. The Civil Rights Movement had started and the vibrations were felt around the world.

On his way, Baldwin stopped over in New York and was involved for awhile in an aborted attempt to stage a dramatic version of his recent novel, *Giovanni's Room.* Once he reached the South he joined the marches there and in Birmingham he walked with Dr. Martin Luther King, Jr., and other non-violent demonstrators for civil rights.

The black kids in the South made a deep impression on his searching mind. It took a great deal of courage to go into white schools, to be spat upon by a mob of hostile white people day after day. But the black students held their heads high and it made Baldwin proud to see them. They obviously believed what Martin Luther King told them: "Love your enemy." And they conducted themselves like heroes.

For many months Baldwin took part in the freedom struggle. Soon however he began to realize he was gaining a name as a "Negro leader." It bothered that region of his mind that was a writer. He had to admit to himself finally that whatever he could do to help break down the walls that kept people prisoners on both sides of the racial nightmare had to be done through his function as a writer.

Thousands of miles away from the racial crisis Baldwin found a place of peace in Istanbul, Turkey, where he could finish his big novel, *Another Country*. On December 10th, 1961, the work was done. He had had a hard time making it the way he wanted it. Sometimes he wasn't even sure what the main idea of the book should be—or if there should be a main idea—and many times he rewrote one section or another.

When Dial brought out *Another Country* in June 1962, it quickly took a high place on the nation-wide bestseller list. But among the critics there were mixed reactions to Baldwin's new work. Some thought it the most powerful novel in years. Others felt that *Another Country* was out of focus and that its author would do better to stick to writing essays. One day the *New York Times* said the book was "strained" and two days later another *Times* review found it "brilliantly and fiercely told." Three days after publication, Dial gave a press reception in Baldwin's honor at Small's Paradise—the author's favorite restaurant in Harlem. It was a celebration to remember: Baldwin did the Twist and everybody seemed in good spirits.

Later Baldwin agreed to go to Africa for *The New Yorker* magazine and write about what he saw and heard and felt in the land of his early ancestors. He took his sister, Gloria Davis, with him. He had been afraid of going to Africa. The fear was difficult to define, but now he discovered, to his pleasant surprise, that all his fears had been for nothing—they both loved Africa from the first moment. They moved along the West Coast enjoying everything they found. In all, they were in Africa ten weeks, and Baldwin was proud of having been taken for an African on many occasions.

After leaving Africa he went back to his retreat in Turkey where he could be alone. He had a lot of work to finish. Meanwhile *The New Yorker* published a piece by Baldwin which they had already accepted before sending him on assignment. It was a 20,000-word essay called "Letter from a Region in My Mind." He was paid $6,500 for it, and when it appeared in the magazine it went over so well that Dial wanted to publish it in book form. The book, titled *The Fire Next Time,* was immediately recognized as one of the important books of the time, and in the United States the name James Baldwin become a household word.

The Fire Next Time stayed high on the bestseller list for forty-one weeks.

Meanwhile, Baldwin had started work on a play called *Blues for Mister Charlie.* The idea for the play came in part from the killing which Medgar Evers, the NAACP worker in Mississippi, had been investigating when he was murdered, and in part from an earlier incident: the killing of a little black boy, Emmett Till, who had whistled at a white woman.

Since receiving a Eugene F. Saxon Memorial Trust Award at the beginning of his career, James Baldwin has been honored by many awards, including a Guggenheim Literary Fellowship, a National Institute of Arts and Letters Fellowship and a Ford Foundation Grant-in-Aid. He was now honored once again. In 1963 he was given a George Polk Memorial Award for "outstanding magazine reporting."

Now, however, if Baldwin wanted to get any work done he definitely had to go far away. So he took off again for Instanbul, where he was able to finish the first act of *Blues for Mister Charlie* before returning to the United States for a speaking tour.

Baldwin remained deeply concerned about the growing racial crisis. Riots broke out in many cities, and almost always police mishandling of incidents caused the outbreaks. Officials of the law were using fire hoses and swinging clubs on black youth. Black people were being shot down in the streets of hundreds of towns and cities and it reminded Baldwin of the time of his father's funeral—the Detroit and Harlem riots of 1943.

Due to an impassionate telegram Baldwin sent to Attorney General Robert F. Kennedy, then head of the Department of

Justice, a famous get-together took place. Kennedy asked Baldwin to round up a group of people to discuss with him the racial crisis and what the Federal government could do about it. Among those Baldwin invited were Harry Belafonte, Lena Horne, Lorraine Hansberry, and Dr. Kenneth Clark. The discussion produced no immediate, tangible results. Kennedy later said that he still believed the Federal government should rely on judicial processes where civil rights cases were concerned rather than interfering directly in a state's affairs.

In his childhood, Baldwin had known a boy who was now a successful photographer, Richard Avedon. Avedon wanted Baldwin to write the text for a book of his photographs, and Baldwin enthusiastically agreed. They called the book *Nothing Personal*.

Finally Baldwin finished the play. *Blues For Mister Charlie* opened on the night of April 23, 1964, at the ANTA Theatre in New York. Baldwin sat in the audience with a very close friend, Mary Painter (to whom he had dedicated his novel, *Another Country*). A lot of sweat and work had gone into making the play a success. Not only Baldwin but also all the actors and other theatre people involved—including the stars, Burgess Meredith and Diana Sands—had put in many long hours. Unfortunately, however, the play was not a success. Even the best reviews were not really good. Some viewers believed that white Americans were not willing to *see* what Baldwin was saying, others that they could not. But the play itself, apart from its message, somehow did not work with audiences. It did run for four months, however, before it finally had to close.

By that time, Baldwin was back in his hideaway in Istanbul, at work on a new novel. (It would be called *Tell Me How Long The Train's Been Gone,* and was published in 1967.) In 1965 he published his first collection of short stories, *Going to Meet the Man*. It contained stories dating back as far as 1948. Although books of short stories don't usually sell well, this book was a success because Baldwin's name was well known.

Over the years Baldwin had built up a very comfortable income from his writing. The days of near-starvation were over. He could afford almost anything material which he wanted. He maintained apartments in New York, Paris and Istanbul.

So he had become a famous writer. But in a way, he had also become a preacher—his original ambition. He had struck a fire in the mind of the nation.

John A. Williams:
The Black Writer
Who Cried I Am

His writing career began when he was about 25. In 1950 he started writing for newspapers, and six years later he published a work of short fiction in a magazine called *Gent*. The way was rough for John A. Williams but by 1969 he had become an outstanding writer. Not that being a famous writer had ever been his goal. He'd simply wanted to write well and to make a living doing what he enjoyed. In 1963, when Williams published his third novel, *Sissie,* he already felt that "Almost without fail, a novel written by a Negro is said to be one of anger, hatred, rage or protest . . .", that "These little tickets deprive that novel of any ability it may have to voice its concern for all mankind, not only Negroes." He said that Negro writers were kept in a sort of literary ghetto, a restriction of which James Baldwin had also complained. Only one Negro writer could emerge at a time, Williams pointed out, and it is unmistakably James Baldwin; no Negro writing in America today can escape his shadow. He replaced Richard Wright, who, in turn, may have replaced Langston Hughes."[1]

By 1970, though he would not exactly replace Baldwin, Williams certainly was long overdue for the recognition he was beginning to get. He had made a "late start." None of his books had sold nearly as well as he might have hoped; he also thought is very sad indeed that publishers were beginning to sign up Negro writers simply because they were Negro. He once heard a publisher say, "Negro stuff is selling well!" (Seven years later, by 1969, it would boom!) But Williams still did not trust the motives for this shift. He felt that a book as a work of art should be judged on its literary merits and not on the nationality of the author.

Already in 1963 Williams saw the "Negro phase" that publishing was beginning to undergo. Earlier, in 1957, when he had only magazine and newspaper publications to his credit and was doing public relations work to make ends meet, an editor sent a note of rejection to Williams' agent stating that the budding author should shift from the "obviously personal experience of being Negro" toward a more financially rewarding type of fiction. This same publisher today is one of the leading proud publishers of "black material."

Williams' struggle before luck came was long and rigorous. He was a working writer for many years before his first book was published. Certainly, more than five years before his first novel, *The Angry Ones,* was published in 1960, he was sending book manuscripts to publishers who were rejecting them, almost always for the wrong reasons. So when in 1963 he found reviewers grouping his novel, *Sissie,* together with new works by, say, James Baldwin and John Oliver Killens, his disapproval was understandable. He was also aware that almost nobody except black writers thought or cared about this fact, which might well be thoughtless bigotry on the part of the reviewer.

From the beginning Williams much admired Chester Himes, a prolific writer of many novels in the naturalist tradition which Williams himself followed. He also admired Richard Wright of whom he wrote: "Many black writers were influenced by Richard Wright, and this, too, I believe, is the sign of an artist, that he is in many ways emulated; the power of his words or the color of his canvas impel others toward their own palettes or pens."[2] And on one of Wright's books he says " I found *Pagan Spain* to be one of Wright's most perceptive books . . . Wright had no particular stake in Spain except as a human being interested in the plight of other human beings.

This marked a very special growth all black writers must move toward—from the burning consideration of the black oppressed to the final consideration of *all* oppressed peoples. In the final analysis, it is this consideration that makes Wright the most important black writer, American, of all times."[3]

Williams himself chose to write novels because they allowed the writer to "explore vigorously the endless delights and agonies . . . only the novel approaches the grandeur, the sweep, the universality of the epic poem."[4] He continued to feel this way as year by year it grew more obvious that the reading public was turning away from fiction toward nonfiction.

Though Williams proved himself early to be an expert short story writer, he considered such writing to be mainly a "training ground for the novelist." In poetry he has not done much, although in 1969 the present writer published one of Williams' poems, "Safari West," in an anthology, *The New Black Poetry*. This poem was rather long, though Williams explained that it was but a small part of a longer incomplete work. It is a very beautiful poem and certainly grew out of reflections on the African slave trade and Williams' own personal experience traveling in Africa.

From the very beginning of his career, Williams showed much more faith in "the article" as a clear, unmistakable weapon for attacking "the cruelty and stupidity of the white American society." Behind him were skilled black writers who had successfully used the same form to reach mainly a large white audience, among them Alain Locke, W.E.B. DuBois, E. Franklin Frazier, John Hope Franklin and J. Saunders Redding.

When James Baldwin read William's second novel *Night Song,* (1961), he said it was a "Remarkably truthful..." book. Baldwin also said that it showed " . . . a painful rage and deep sympathy."

In 1967 Williams published his fourth novel, *The Man Who Cried I Am.* It became a bestseller. The critics praised it. The *San Francisco Examiner* said it was "The most powerful novel about blacks since Ralph Ellison's *Invisible Man."*

At that time John A. Williams was 41 years old. Born John

Alfred Williams on December 5, 1925, in Hinds County, near Jackson, Mississippi, his life had been filled so far with not only ups and downs but much travel and love and work as well. William's mother, Ola Mae Jones, was 20 when he was born and his father, John Henry Williams, was 23. The couple had been living in Syracuse, New York. John Henry Williams took his wife back down South to Hinds County, her birthplace, because she was pregnant with her first child. It was a custom of her people and of her time that her firstborn should be born in the place where she herself had been born.

"I can remember at least four different homes," Williams says, "from the time I was an infant until I went into the Navy at 17½. The only school changes that came were those necessitated by the class you were in . . . There were other black students, but we were a decided minority then. I wasn't very good at most subjects. Terrible in arithmetic."[5]

It was while in the Navy that he first read the work of Chester Himes and began thinking of being a writer. After his discharge in 1947, at the age of 21, he married Carolyn Clopton and that year their first son, Gregory, was born. In 1951 they had their second child, Dennis, and by 1952 Williams was working two jobs: He had held many disappointing jobs before and now he worked for the Onandaga County Welfare Department in Syracuse, which he found interesting. He also worked on a part-time basis for a public relations firm. Meanwhile he was attending classes at Syracuse University and in 1950 earned a Bachelor of Arts Degree; in 1951 he finished graduate school and was already writing a lot on his own. One of the first magazines to print his work was *Neurotica*. He was then already working on *The Angry Ones,* which he finished in 1955. Soon he moved to New York City.

From 1954 to 1955 Williams worked for the Columbia Broadcasting System (CBS). This was his second public relations job and here he covered "special events"; but he quit for what appeared to be a better job at Comet Press Books, a vanity house. He became its publicity director and later said it was "a heart-breaking hustle".[6] The following year he became self-employed, editing and publishing the *Negro Market Newsletter*. However in 1957 he went to work as assistant to the publisher at Abelard-Schuman, a New York City publishing firm; then in that year he became Director of Information to the American Committee on Africa, where he worked for eight months. In 1958, as a correspondent for *Ebony* and *Jet*, Williams left for Europe.

When he returned in 1959 he accepted a job as a fund-raiser for the New York Chapter of the National Committee for a Sane Nuclear Policy. Though probably under surveillance by the Dodd Committee, Williams put together the biggest protest ever against nuclear testing, which was the broadest peace delegation so far.

Unlike the publisher of his first novel, Ace Books, Inc., the publisher of his second novel, Farrar, Straus & Giroux, was mainly a hardback book publisher. They brought out *Night Song* with pride and the *Chicago Tribune* said that it reflected "The truth, cut close to the core . . . ." In this writer's opinion it is Williams' best novel to date.

Meanwhile, he continued to write and to publish short fiction and articles in magazines such as *Swank* and *The Urbanite*. In 1962 he edited and wrote an introduction to a paperback anthology, *The Angry Black*, published by Lancer Books. But 1962 was really Williams' year of "the Farce de Rome."

The date was January 23. His telephone rang and he answered and the voice informed him that he'd been chosen to receive a Fellowship to the American Academy in Rome. It would be for the year October 1962-October 1963. The caller wanted to know if Williams would accept. Of course, he would accept. He was very excited and felt for the first time his talent was being noticed. '*Wow!* the Prix de Rome!' Now, maybe he'd be able to shake his feeling of not really being a writer. Perhaps being a writer wasn't "an afliction" after all.

Soon, a formal letter from the Academy came, but the sentence in it that caught Wiliams' eye was: " . . . subject to the approval of the American Academy in Rome."[7] The letter was signed by Mr. Douglas Moore, President of the American

Academy of Arts and Letters (AAAL). The letter also explained that the grant money was a total of $3,500; he went for his first interview concerning the appointment on February 15th. Interviewed by Mr. Richard A. Kimball, Director of the Academy in Rome, Williams left Kimball's office with an uncertain feeling.

Several days later Williams received a letter from the "parent body" of the American Academy in Rome: the National Institute of Arts and Letters. "You will shortly hear from the American Academy in Rome," it said, "stating that the recommendation of the American Academy of Arts and Letters that you be elected a Fellow was not approved."[8] However, said the letter, Williams was being offered a grant of $2,000 from the NIAL for his "contribution" to American literature. On March 2nd he received a letter from Richard A. Kimball's secretary saying: "We regret to inform you that another candidate also recommended by the American Academy of Arts and Letters was awarded the Fellowship in creative writing."[9] Nothing else.

Naturally Williams wanted to know what had really happened. The publisher of *Night Song* decided to write and ask. ". . . We insist that some explanation is owed him, and us as his publishers, as to why this honor which was to be conferred upon him was so suddenly withdrawn."[10] Of the three final candidates for the Fellowship, John A. Williams had been chosen without question over the others. Douglas Moore's March 14th response to the publisher was brief: "My notification to Mr. Williams was premature, and I apologize to him although he was first on our list as originally submitted."[11]

In any case, Williams was baffled. Was it because of some political juggling? Had he became the victim of racial prejudice? Could someone have something against his political work with the National Committee for a Sane Nuclear Policy?

He strongly suspected that Kimball had a lot to do with the change in the decision. Anyway, the American Academy in Rome had chosen another person, although it wasn't supposed to have the power to do that. Traditionally it used its power, if necessary, to decide on a rejection.

Though he badly needed the money Williams decided to turn down the $2,000 "consolation" prize. "I feel now that were I to accept the award," he wrote Douglas Moore, "it would be tacit agreement that no explanation (for my rejection) was due me. I regret to inform you, therefore, that I must decline the award."[12] Moore's only response was assurance that Williams' name would be removed from the ceremonial program. But Williams asked that his name be left on the ceremonial and that his letter rejecting the award be read aloud to the audience.

In a letter to Williams the President of the Rome Academy assured him that nothing racial was involved in the decision to give the award to poet Alan Dugan. Dugan would get it rather than Williams, President Michael Rapuano said, because the poet "would profit more from the year in Rome..."[13] than Williams would.

Williams turned down the grant and that made him a "bad boy"; meanwhile, nothing about this episode had reached any of the big newspapers. Naturally Williams wondered why. At the ceremonial Malcolm Cowley, President of the National Institute of Arts and Letters, spoke. He said Williams turned down the grant offered because of some "misapprehension". But the letter which Williams had asked to be read was not read. If the "second choice" winner, Alan Dugan, had not spoken out on the issue it might have died at that point. Dugan said the "painful mess" *could have* been avoided. Why hadn't the judges remained firm in their choice of Williams? Williams felt it was brave of Dugan to have brought it out into the open. That took courage. Newsmen around the world suddenly took notice and there were many congratulations for Dugan. After Dugan, Malcolm Cowley spoke again, saying there would be a "review" of the inter-workings between these institutions.

The incident, by the way, did lead to a crisis between the American Academy and the Rome Academy. After they broke off their relations, Williams accepted the $2,000 grant.

1963 was a big and busy year for Williams. On a special assignment for *Holiday* magazine, he traveled around the United States. His purposes was to try to get a sense of its people and then write about his experiences. Once the *Holiday* trip was behind him he got to work. He observed: "I felt upon my return that I had changed, perhaps even grown . . . I had had to reach the conclusion that man, as I knew him best, in America, was not basically good, as is always suggested, but evil in the primitive, possessive, and destructive sense. I knew good people existed; I had been fortunate in meeting many of them . . ."[14]

He also completed a picture book, *Africa: Her History, Lands and People,* published by Cooper Square Publishers. In it Williams drew on his experience gained while working for the American Committee on Africa.

In 1964 he went to Africa then spent six months in Europe; when he returned home he revised his *Africa* book for a new edition. Again in 1965 Williams went to Africa, this time for *Newsweek* magazine. However, *Newsweek* used only part of one story he wrote for them. They showed no interest in Williams' story of Malcolm X in Lagos.

Williams was also working for the Forum Service News, which had its central office in London. He also finished two films for the National Education Television network. The work was done in Nigeria, and he himself was reporter, script writer and narrator. One film was titled, "The History of the Negro People: Omowale," and the other, "The Child Returns Home." This represented more hardwork than he cared to mention.

During this time a motion picture company made and released a film version of Williams' novel, *Night Song.* The title of the movie was "Sweet Love Bitter," starring Dick Gregory, Diana Varsi and Don Murray.

Williams' report for *Holiday* also appeared now, in both hardbound and paperback editions from The New American Library and it sold reasonably well. Meanwhile, he was at work on a new novel, a big one. He was also revising the *Africa* book for the third time.

In 1967 Cooper Square published Williams' revised edition of his early anthology, *The Angry Black,* under the title, *Beyond The Angry Black.* The same year his biggest novel, both in size and reception, *The Man Who Cried I Am,* was published by Little, Brown & Company, and quickly became a bestseller. Its popular success was at least matched by its critical success.

William was still traveling a great deal. He'd already visited Belgium, Cameroun, Canada, Congo, Cyprus, Denmark, Egypt, Ethiopia, France, Germany, Ghana, Great Britain, Greece, Israel, Italy, Mexico, The Netherlands, Nigeria, Portugal, Senegal, Spain, The Sudan, Sweden, and the Virgin Islands, where in the summer of 1968 he was guest lecturer at the College of the Virgin Islands.

He had married a second time in 1965 a young woman named Lorrain Isaac and now born to them was a baby son they called Adam. 1968 was also the beginning of more and more work for Williams. Already he was planning two more novels, one of which was about black soldiers in World War II. The other novel was finished first and published the following year under the title, *Sons of Darkness, Sons of Light.*

John Williams and I met in Philadelphia in December, 1968, while working with so-called emotionally disturbed boys at the Pennsylvania Advancement School. The first chance John and I had to talk was during lunch break, which we took in a bar-restaurant across from the school.

At the time John had been working on *Sons of Darkness, Sons of Light* and just finished a tremendous series of articles for the *Saturday Evening Post* which they turned down because they disagreed with his outlook on the origins of Negro leadership—one topic of the series. I remember our conversation centered around this and also my own work. I was finishing *All-Night Visitors* (which at that time was called "The Women") and was a little worried about fiinding a publisher. It seemed such a difficult thing to do even with an "acceptable" book manuscript. "It's mainly luck," was John's feeling. (Later, in New York, he set up an appointment for me to see an editor named Ginsberg at Putnam. The editor rejected my novel within a week, saying he found the characters uninteresting.)

Except for breakfast together one morning at his apartment, and a drink together on another occasion, John and I did not see each other for many weeks.

Then, along with June Jordan, in 1969, I read some of my poems at the Guggenheim Museum and invited John to both the reading and the party that followed. The party took place in William Meredith's sister's Manhattan apartment and June had invited some of her friends, too. It was here that I first expressed to John the idea of writing these words. He seemed to like the notion and within a few days I started making notes.

Notes

1. "The Literary Ghetto," *Saturday Review*, April 20, 1963.
2. "On Wright, Wrong and Black Reality," *Negro Digest*, Vol. XVIII No. 2, December, 1968.
3. Ibid.
4. "The Negro In Literature Today," *Ebony*, September, 1963.
5. From personal letter dated 5/27/69.
6. From personal letter dated July 28, 1969.
7. "We Regret To Inform You," in *Flashbacks*, New York, Doubleday, 1973, p. 358.
8. Ibid., p. 360.
9. Ibid., p. 360.
10. Ibid., p. 361.
11. Ibid., p. 361.
12. Ibid., p. 364.
13. Ibid., p. 364.
14. *This Is My Country Too*. New American Library, 1965.

Willard Motley:
Vague Ghost After the Father

I never knew Willard Motley in any real sense; I met him only once and he wrote to me from Mexico only once, asking me to meet him at his mother's house on the west side of Chicago to talk and have beer, during that summer of 1960 when he was planning to come home.

We didn't meet that way, though. It was a very uncomfortable meeting, unpleasant for everybody in the room—Archibald Motley, Hugh Grayson, Willard and myself. We were all standing, suddenly, in the kitchen of the Motley home. (I had gotten to know Archibald fairly well earlier, first because we both had paintings in Gayles Gallery, and second because I had talked with him several times to get information on his career, in order to build a magazine article, which was accepted by *Black Orpheus,* in Nigeria, but never published.)

Relatively speaking, Willard Motley had been somewhat important to me. His books, *Knock On Any Door* and *We Fished All Night* (not so much *Let No Man Write My Epitaph,* though I read it half-heartedly), had a strange impact on me. When I was in high school and had read everything by Richard Wright, I turned to other black writers, among them Willard Motley. A kind of ghost among Negro writers, he was. In those first two big, raw, clumsy books, I found something vital and real. They were valid for me—though Motley was hardly considered a respected and "serious" writer by most black and white critics. But I could look at the *bulk* of his work and, from a writer's point of view, get inspiration. *All that work!* God it was amazing! I used to open them and read at random. He really knew a lot about the social habits of Italians, Poles, Jews, and the bums of West Madison Street.

But then he lived a long time among those poor Italians, Poles, Jews, and bums. Archibald, his brother, a big, impressive man with skin the color of peach, with eyes like two soft lights, a goat's T of hair on his chin, stood up from where we were sitting at the dining room table and demonstrated for me how carefully he had to walk across the floor boards in Willard's basement apartment, during Willard's West Madison Street days, because mud was oozing up between the boards onto Archibald's shoes. Willard Motley actually lived in *that* kind of poverty while writing *Knock On Any Door*. He *chose* to live that way. The manuscript was finally shipped off in a crate—it was that big—only to be rejected for being too long and too crude. Archibald said his younger brother had baffled them all when he moved out of the comfort of the family home to live in such squalor. But Archibald came to understand very soon that it was something that "Brother" *had* to do.

I remember the nervous pitch of Willard Motley's thin, soft voice; the almost effeminate way his mouth formed words, which reminded me also of Truman Capote's mouth forming sounds. Norman Ross was interviewing Motley once on his VIP show, and the novelist couldn't seem to get his voice above a whisper. Ross asked. "Why do you write about people around West Madison Street rather than about Negroes?" (i.e., as other Negro writers do). Motley said softly, "I find the plight of the people on West Madison Street *more* urgent." I almost fell off my chair. There he was, sitting there in his white silky-looking suit, like a butterscotch-colored South American tobacco-inspector, saying some shit like *that!* I turned to Grayson, who was also watching it, and I couldn't see his face, only the interior of his mouth—he was laughing so hard. Even my wife, in the kitchen making coffee, fell out.

As I say, I saw nothing in *Let No Man Write My Epitaph* and didn't even bother to try to read *Let Noon Be Fair*. Even if the latter is in some way worth reading or is good or is better than anything he wrote prior to it, I probably will never know ... I mean, by the time the novel came out, which was, I think, after his death in 1965 of 1966, I was no longer interested in Willard Motley. I wasn't impressed by all that work anymore. I was moving on. Besides, I was turning away from fiction in those days toward psychology, anthropology, history, etc.

Another thing. The name Richard Wright was a very evil word—or so I gathered—in the Motley home. Archibald was quick to let me know that! The verbal energy with which he put down *Black Boy* and *Native Son* almost turned the pages of my notebook!

Willard Motley died still being put to the side by critics who studied Negro fiction. In any evaluation of American Negro literature he is to be considered. Usually, however, he is treated with as much disrespect as is Frank Yerby. But unlike Richard Wright or William Demby, both excellent craftsmen, Yerby and Motley turned out the kind of lusty or sensational material that brought to them considerable wealth. (And Yerby, of course, is still at it.)

Frank London Brown:
Reckless Enough to be a Man

Frank London Brown is a relatively unimportant Negro American novelist who died of cancer of the blood before he had a chance to establish himself as a figure in literature and a voice for black liberation. He said one night at the South Side Community Art Center that the race issue was the most important thing in the world to him. In his only novel,* *Trumbull Park,* he says, "... It takes something to be reckless enough to be a man, especially if you're colored."

I am looking at the yellowed pages of a manuscript I wrote eight years ago, in Chicago, up on North Clark Street in a little office frantically given to the uncertain business of publishing a new middle-class-oriented "slick" magazine aimed at Negroes. The article is titled "Frank London Brown: A Fine New American Talent." The name of the magazine that never got beyond the first issue is not important; in itself it was ,a failure at what it attempted to do: it did not reach people.

There was a rather pleasant black man, a Mr. W.M., who first urged me to come to work for the new publication. It just happened that, at that time, I was putting together somes notes on Frank Brown. He looked over the material, was impressed and promised me "the moon." So, I started going over to the North Side. (Richard Wright, thirty years before had started going over to the North Side, too. But for different reasons.)

---

* A second novel, *The Myth Maker* (Path Press, Inc., 1969), was published posthumously.

The editor and publisher, whom I soon met, was a short, handsome, rather arrogant guy whose brown face obviously threw to you immediate signs that he thought himself important and clever. He had previously gained small attention after publishing (out of his own pocket) a hardback book of Negro personalities, and now this magazine, call it *New World,* was his slow brainstorm.

So many of the people *he* had grown up with had become "somebody" and he, too, meant to make the grade. At least three close friends had invested heavily in this proposed magazine. Three telephones had been installed, and we had an air-conditioner. A plump lovely soul sister was there every day or almost every day to answer the telephone; and there were guys, mostly connected to the subscription department, easing in and out of the office, not really serious about anything except looking pretty, not really selling subscriptions but just stopping in to breathe the "air" of the place between cruises across the baking hot pavement of the city in the Cadillac or in one of the other good-looking cars. There was a good excuse for driving all the way to the South Side, though: the printer's shop was located out there.

But Frank Brown's tender, dark face was somewhere in my mind. I can see the publisher and managing editor of *New World* (or *Colored World*) now, sitting at *my* desk. I am standing to the side, looking down into his grinning face. The hairs of his mustache curl over onto his lip. I think he is ugly. But I know *he* thinks he is God's gift. Let him think what he needs to think. He is talking into the phone to Frank. "Hi, there, Frank old boy, how're you? Remember when you pulled that girl's pigtails, what was her name? Haha haha! ha ha ha! . . . Yeah, remember that? at DuSable High . . . Yeah, man, those were the days! We were young then, Frank. Age slipping up on us, Frank. What can we do? Say—we got a story down here about you! Yeah! A story! About you and your book! Who wrote it? A young guy named Clarence Major. Yeah. That's right. Yeah, he *said* you had met . . . What kind of magazine will it be? Good question. Well—" and he went on to explain it all very extensively.

But I was thinking about Frank Brown then with a little envy because he had managed to do the one thing in life I wanted most: he had sold a novel and could hold a published copy in his hand. Look at it. The physical reality of an arrangement of his own ideas and feelings. A thing that many other people read and respond to. They could hold the same reality in *their* hands. And it would be his reality! Oh. I envied Frank so much then. It was a way of admiring him. What I felt did not stifle me.

I am thinking about Frank Brown now, eight years later. Through we met only twice we had mutual "friends" such as the bookdealer, William H. Harper, and the poet, Margaret Danner. I remember hearing over the radio in 1964 that Frank had died and that he was only about thirty-five or so. I was sitting at my typewriter with a tremendous novel in progress and with no hope of ever getting it published. The news of Brown's death left me droopy with my own desperate situation. (But I got myself into another state of mind and that is another story.)

If you look at it in a conventional way, by European-American standards, you might say Frank London Brown wrote a first-rate novel which had all the qualities a novel "should" have. The development and growth of the characters, though stereotyped, were good—in the chosen context and by the standard black writing was being subjected to in those days. Brown had an easy style. A sense of humor. A fast-moving prose. Obviously he learned a lot from Richard Wright and Chester Himes, themselves two very different writers.

The hero of *Trumbull Park,* Buggy Martin, is a super martyr whom the publisher (so I'm told) thought a little *too* heroic! It is the story of a black family that moves into an all-white suburb of Chicago, Trumbull Park. They are unwanted, naturally. The male head of the house has a police escort to and from work, at first, because of threats from, and attacks on his property by, his neighbors. But our hero soon bravely

101

abandons this law enforcement protection, deciding to go it alone, to face openly and independently the problem of his neighbors' hostility. He is somewhat like one of those American pioneers characters in the corny flicks who settle land in hostile Indian territory.

Frank Brown experienced something like what happens in the novel itself. The Trumbull Park episode, I remember, was played up in the Chicago newspapers. I think it was around 1945. So Frank began with a popular subject and something he had first-hand knowledge of. When the book came out the publisher actually promoted it by rehashing the old news story. I saw copies of *Trumbull Park* on newspaper stands—where you never see hardback books (and it was never in paperback).

Margaret Danner who in those days was proud of having once been an editor of *Poetry,* where she met many great white poets) used to talk a lot about Frank Brown. But I knew her only slightly better than I knew him. She told many little "in" stories about how the book got published, how the publisher held it "up in the air" for about a year before making a decision to publish.

Though Brown's life was short, it was rich. Right after the publication of his novel he went to work as a writer for *Ebony* and produced two interesting profiles, one of Mahalia Jackson and the other of Thelonious Monk. Before he wrote Trumbull Park he had been a jazz musician himself and loved music. He was, in those times, corresponding with Alan Paton, the white South African writer who encouraged him to put the Trumbull Park experiences to paper. Born in Kansas City, he grew up in Chicago. He was in Cuba observing and writing what he saw when Castro overthrew the Batista regime. Like man, you're an intellectual, how come you talk hipcat jive, the *Chicago Defender* seemed to be asking him in an inteview, and Brown's simple answer to a question that didn't deserve an answer was, Like I'm a Negro and feel it.

Brown had attended Roosevelt University. There was this white boy I knew who was also going there, later, and putting out a literary magazine, in which Frank and I both published.

102

Robin Cuscaden called his publication, *Vigil*. The piece of fiction by Brown that appeared in *Vigil* he later read to a small group, in which I took part, at the South Side Community Art Center. It was about a family in a burning building and the mother could save only one of her twins. She had to choose between them. To pull one from the burning wreckage would mean the death of the other and she could not possibly pull them both safely. So the story is about this mental agony.

The last time I saw Frank London Brown was at an art exhibition in Lake Meadows. With him was his tall, elegant light-skinned wife. He seemed very happy and was making plans to go to Israel.

These yellow pages are as stale and obscure as Frank Brown's short career. He will remain a minor writer occupying a small place in the literary history of black Chicago.

Eldridge Cleaver:
And White Writers

In his essay, "The White Race and Its Heroes," Eldridge Cleaver talks *to* white folks. "Tolerate me." Being an Ofay Watcher. Move talk exist, "concealed in the shadows" of a penal system in dream. Says his "intention was not necessarily to sprinkle salt over anyone's wounds."

Transformed by the teachings of Malcolm X from a believer in Elijah Muhammad to a seer of the whites of the eyes of whites. Say "imperialist." Behind one is " devil," and "beast." The joy spreads through the weariness.

Diversity yes. But a common bond among blacks: Break the "ofays'" hold, he moves out into the open. We talk in terms of light and shadow. The universal and the particular. Or the particular.

Yet he finds the generation gap "deeper" than the "struggle between the races." Behind the civil rights protest "the white race has lost its heroes." Yeah, they come down front, exposed, one at a time under the lights, stripped " villains" and "arch-villains." Kids disown them. Kids run naked through their dreams eating wild flowers! The search for the central power in the self to be well. He keeps looking.

White nationalism was not the word but certainly the underbelly. Things thoughts feelings crawl around in the low areas where the self's meanings struggle. Group survival. The way we define human being: a social animal. One's white life is firmly established in the network system that gives one the totem security to go on "rooted in the myth of white supremacy."

You don't know when Cleaver wrote the white race article but 1968 was *Soul on Ice* time. That is ages ago in the fast reel. Would he say today that the white youth is in the "vanguard"?

The coldest thing one can do is write a dated political article. You have to keep looking in. The energy the whites got, the fire they picked up was black. Its medium was the civil rights struggle. Before that, slavery. Women, white women discovered *themselves* accidentally while fighting for the black man's freedom. The feminist movement was born. Look at the impetus of other movements. The Beat Generation and white poets and writers. Here we are finally at our chosen subject and its overlapping borders.

Unrest. Radical roots. Trace even a literary thing back socially politically to the paradox of a free white country holding a black slave. Revolution at its roots. Equal rights and doubletalk: the madness is larger than the man.

And even back to Europe and logic versus the Dark and Feeling. Many ways to say it.

The white poets and novelists of the 1960s got a whiff of this Dark and Feeling. They took it, like white musicians had taken black music from the gutbucket, and gave it their own cultural framework. Ain't nothing wrong with this. I've said it for years: you get your energy where you can. Nabokov calls it inspiration and that is not tasteless.

Somebody, I forget who, describes a person with a beard and rumpled clothes and sandals and bongo drums as a beat. Is this the same person Cleaver calls the master's child? A rebellious attitude. Is this a fair description of the hip white, the beat writer? The minute somebody tries to write a book calling it "Youth and Alienation" the potential reader's willingess and goodwill crumbles away, soft earth beneath the foot. Large sweeping strokes do just that, they simply sweep. The particular has no meaning. I mean, I can say Paul Blackburn wrote bland poetry; whether or not I mean it means *more* than saying, The Beat Generation was a put-on.

The 1950s. The Beats were really up at the end of the 50s and early 60s. Authority was worried just a little. The Drug culture was on the rise. Blacks were still somehow back there behind everything: the cause, but blamed or given credit only when the result was a drag. See all this heavy disenchantment spreading through the early 1970s? It came from well-composed minds. People go mad only because they begin from something called logic. You have to be saved. And the way is through the lingo of magic understanding and a trust in the Dark and Feeling. They interchange.

You can call it political *action* if you wanna but you get turned around, trapped in match and the spell of Rap. Dark and Feeling have moved nations since the beginning of man's *re*action to woman's awesome ability to give birth to man *and* woman. It's how civilization began.

The beatnik did not seem political. The white poets and writers of the 1960s (or late 50s early 60s) were not an unreasonable bunch. Yet they were, in their subjective way, strungout social commentators. There is no greater militant than a satirist. You say this at night in bed to your wife. Ferlinghetti, oh yeah, from the beginning made clear his political stand. He could be beat *and* committed at the same time. Tall droopy corn is a good way of saying it, his words. Also, "a four-dollar piece of lettuce." But Kerouac tore his own ass. Remember *On The Road*? And the lilac evening? And the romanticized "Negro"? The white man wishing he was black? I don't believe it. Look at what he became! Allen Ginsberg's protest poem, "Howl," is the political meat of the Beats. And Seymour Krim romanticizing not only blacks but Hemingway and you name it. Actually it's harmless stuff. We can live with it. Images. Shapes and forms. People go around and change. Except right at dead center.

Copouts. Dropouts. Potheads. Hopheads. Popart. Opart. Renaming things and ideas, the evolution of contact, speech, writing. The eyes change what they see. Black slang became the tongue. Just as the downhome white church imitated the downhome black church, the black speech secrets got out in the open and were copped by the mainstream voice, and the media and Dark and Feeling became white. See the word Hip. See millions of other things beginning with the letters of the alphabet.

Those young whites who were not into the Beat (and later Hippie) thing either got into the path of their parents or became "magnetically" (as Cleaver says) attached to the Negro revolt. What a phrase. Or they finally caught on to Malcolm's idea that they should work their own neighborhoods, to try to do something about white racism. The big enemy. This is background to white poets and novelists of the late 50s and early 60s (or the 1960's). But the implication is that the artists were the least effective of the new white persons, called The Youth. By 1965 the hippie thing was spreading. Flower children in Tompkins Square Park and in San Francisco and Berkeley. Against this background what sort of poetry did Ginsberg Ferlinghetti Corso Blackburn McClure write? Each different. So labels fall off, without meaning. The New American Poetry is an illusion at sea. That remarkable ability the hip critics spoke of is a dubious property. It always is in any age among any people. (Black writers turn out a lot of fluff, too.) But one thing hangs in there: the Dark and the Feeling at the roots. The struggle against Europe's sensibility and its principle, Logic.

"America," the United States, had to be shown that the Devil was a Joyous Soul. A good guy. A fella from Brooklyn or Harlem who could dance and think *too*. This is where the white poets caught on. The Devil was not necessarily the evil spirit white cultures said he was. Around the North Pole some people for a long time have belived *white* is a symbol of evil. The Feeling may change its rhythm but not its intent.

Few writers could embrace both a personal approach and a political position and made them work as one. Hardly any succeeded. The only way to be revolutionary is to begin from one's deepest motivations. But this idea was not on the back

108

of the cards the artists carried. The Dark may change its shape but not its meaning.

In 1960 Elias Wilentz (in *The Beat Scene*—Corinth) offers information on this white movement. John Clellon Holmes takes himself to be the name-giver. Jack Kerouac is the starter. But does it mean "beatitude" or is this an afterthought? After the facts. And Norman Mailer, in his tracings to the cool hipster, sounds like he has a mouth full of words words words doing each other in.

Ironically the label comes from *Life* and *Time* who, early in the game, picked up the vibes and called the movement "beat"—in the media's traditional effort both to catch shock-value news and to bring the stray kids back home to dullness and deadness. They had wandered away into the Dark and gotten a touch of the Feeling. It was too much. *Life* lampooned them. And soon the weakest poets among them *believed* the image.

These weak ones called themselves Beat Poets and acted out crazy skits, running around feeling like they were into something. Clowns jumping up and down for attention. Trying to cash in on the thing of the moment. The real ones were back there in the shadows thinking and doing their work. They survived and are still read today—maybe tomorrow too. To name a few, Gary Snyder Gilbert Sorrentino Robert Creeley—who else? Others surely.

Perverted glamour? That is the way a segment of middle-class white America defined it. Jazz records and a copy of *Howl* somebody once said. Sexual excess and drugs. They moved from coast to coast as though the middle were not there. (Now their descendents live in communes in the middle.) What little clarity there was fades.

Yet some things remain clear. The qualities usually found in academic verse and fiction were rejected—more firmly in theory than in practice. Also, the best poets critics novelists of these years worked outside the Beat circle. People like Margaret Randall, John Berryman, Walter Lowenfels, Kenneth Patchen, Gil Orlovitz, W.S. Merwin, Marvin Bell and Sandra

109

Hochman. Their kind was not into superhip and supercool. The struggle to write honestly was large enough a task without wasting time playing games.

Soon evolved The New York Poets. Another type to which poor spirits jumped for security. The weak ones need movement always: they can't make it on their own. Originally this group consisted of persons like John Ashbery, Frank O'Hara and Kenneth Koch. Most of them had started publishing their stuff in the early 50s, actually. But they got no notice until they got together under the slogan. The Living Theatre and the Artists Theatre were the New York scenes. This was early on, the 50s still. Edward Field and Barbara Guest and James Schuyler. New names came onto the New York Poets membership list: Tom Clark, Michael Brownstein, Ted Berrigan, Mark Strand, Ron Padgett, Aram Saroyan, Charles Simic. But all white poets living in New York are not identified with the New York Poets scene— Diane Wakoski and Michael Benedikt being two examples.

Neither can good writers be defined along geographical lines—certainly not in terms of groups (despite the fact that people move together up or down). Stuart Perkoff and Ron Loewinsohn and David Meltzer were late arriving on the San Francisco scene, possibly because they were busy elsewhere. Gary Snyder was in Japan, and when he was in this country he was mostly in the woods to himself. The wise ones stay away from fads.

A prime mover in the white literary upsurge was LeRoi Jones (later known as Imamu Amiri Baraka, the Black Nationalist). Jones (and Ted Joans) were the two main black poets making that scene. At least they got more attention. But how did the Dark and the Feeling hit them, what did it mean to them? Somebody may yet uncover that confusion.

These white poets and novelists said all kinds of words attempting to define their own directions. Emotions, says Michael McClure. William Burroughs says, Cutup. Jack Kerouac says Bebop. Ferlinghetti says commitment. Robert Duncan says The Open Composition. Creeley says, the Word itself.

110

But the underlying mood and impulse is rebellion. Its central force it not very clear, There is hardly any direction. But it *is* rebellion. You might call it reaction. Something new, folks, was in the air. D.H. Lawrence had had his day and left his passion. Henry Miller had stretched out in a word jungle on fire. The darkness is heavily diffused at its center and the feelings we get reading this stuff are wide. Lowenfels says, "Now everybody wants to say his last words, paint his last pictures, write his last symphony."*

Had a new demotic literature appeared in the United States? I think not. (I like the deep roots of good poems in books by dudes like Galway Kinnell—who was never a bigmouth.) I think the noise was greater than the quality. True, nobody was trying to justify the crap their forefathers and mothers put down as The Way and nobody was grinding that many dumb political axes. I said it once, I say it again: it was diffused and without central force. And who can argue with it? The here and now was the meat and bread. Dissent but not dissenters? A lot of it was too stupid for words. Unity. Matter. Form. Make it new. Things that people simply repeat but news was made.

---

* *In a Time of Revolution*. Random House, 1969.

Part Four

Work with the Universe: An Interview With Clarence Major And Victor Hernandez Cruz

Victor was upstairs in his smoking jacket, purple; it was summer and we were guests in a pleasant big house on a hill with a view of a lake through small trees. I called Victor down to meet Walt Shepperd, editor of the Nickel Review, *and another guy whose name I forgot. Victor, a two-day guest, and I, a two-week guest, at Cazenovia College's Summer Institute on Black Literature, were ready to talk with somebody outside that circle. It was September, 1969, and my heart was broken but slowly mending.*

SHEPPERD: Clarence, in your anthology, *The New Black Poetry,* are you giving us, by your selection of poets, standards for the definition of a black aesthetic?

MAJOR: What I've had to come to realize is that the question of a black aesthetic is something that really comes down to an individual question. It seems to me that if there is a premise in an artist's work, be he black or white, that it comes out of his work, and therefore out of himself. Or herself. I think that it's also true with *form.* It has to be just that subjective. I don't see any objective way of dealing with the work an artist does, solely along racial lines. Black poets, for instance, are going in many different directions. There are so many forces at work.

SHEPPERD: If we could expand this question to include your book, Victor, *Snaps,* it seems, is poetry that the cat on the corner, particularly the young, can identify with easily. Do you see the emergence of an aesthetic of the streets, perhaps an aesthetic of the oppressed?

CRUZ: The poems in *Snaps* were written in a period when that was more or less what I was coming out of. I used those experiences just like any poet has done in the past. I don't like to say that my work is a part of a new thing that can be identified or pinpointed so that now I can have an umbrella over me or something because here I am in Cazenovia and I should be able to write poems about this. I feel that the writer—a black writer or a Puerto Rican writer—should have just as much right to talk about the universe and how it started as any other writer. I think that some of the people who are into this black writing thing really complicate it to the point where you've got to conform to it and if you don't you're sup-posed to be doing something unnatural. I think a writer should use his total spectrum and, no matter what the situation, he should be able to come out with his own thing. I'm Puerto Rican, but when I was on the airplane coming over here there was no Puerto Rican, there was just me up there in the air, and I could create out of that. I could create out of anything, and I think it's wrong to say that because you're black or Puerto Rican you can't use the whole universe as your field.

MAJOR: That's something that I really began working on with these people in Cazenovia. They're at this conference to try to learn how to put together a Black Studies course, to go back to their black students and teach Black Lit. And like they're sitting there man, really expecting to learn how the black experience and therefore Black Lit is special and dif-ferent.

They're expecting to be let into some kind of deep dark secret. Like, "tell us what it is . . . we have to know . . . what is this special thing, this experience of yours that we can't penetrate . . . what is it?" They really are so convinced that these problems are real; all this shit is in their minds. They can quote Don Quixote and get through it right away. They never lived in Spain and it would be a very strange place for any of them, and yet they can get through Don Quixote on a human level. And I think they could get through a lot of Black Lit if they didn't have these social hangups created by outside forces.

SHEPPERD: Let's talk about those forces for a minute. Victor mentioned black writers complicating their own scene. But you've both had experience with the big publishing houses; don't they have rubber stamps for the book jackets that say "bitter," "angry," "oppressed"? Don't the publishing companies really push you into that bag anyway, or at least try to?

CRUZ: Well a woman in *Negro Digest* mentioned that she couldn't understand why my book was published by Random House. But I don't know, publishing seems better than it used to be. Most people who are in publishing seem eager to get black writers. I would have the same approach to the publishers no matter who they were. Today, especially in poetry, one of the most important thing is to get it out there. And anybody into poetry knows how hard it is to get it out there.

MAJOR: Along the same line, about the psychology of publishers. I had lunch with an editor not long ago and she's considering work by a young black poet, one of the poets in my anthology. He had submitted a manuscript of poems and she really dug them. She really thought they were great. But she couldn't possibly consider it or recommend them to her publisher *because* there's nothing there in the work to indicate that the poems were written by a *black* poet. And she says they can't possibly run on each page a photograph of the poet. And the assumption is, they would *have* to . . . if they published it. She said *that*. "We can't possibly run a photo of him on each page." This is an editor, a person who can make decisions, sitting right there and saying that kind of shit!

CRUZ: This is the same kind of thing that happens with a black publishing company. They'll put you in a bag too. It will probably be quite some time before poets can stand on their own worth no matter what they're talking about. I think that Clarence's book, *All-Night Visitors,* is a milestone for a different thing in black writing. In the past some of the black writers have dealt with sex, for example, in a much different way.

MAJOR: In other words, it is not a Christian book. That's why a lot of people won't be able to get through it.

CRUZ: It's a *book,* man, it stands by itself, and you really couldn't go around trying to relate it to a course.

MAJOR: The people at this conference are having a bitch of a time with it, by the way. It's required reading. But before I got there they were all like in the dorm whispering to each other about it. Probably reading the sexy parts. They were questioning my motives. Some thought the book was a put-on. A number of these people are over 60 years old. Two of them are nuns. Anyway, we finally got into discussion of *All-Night Visitors.* I ran it down and gave them my impression of it and they were really *relieved!* Some of them said, like, "I'm really glad you told me what you were trying to *say* because it really puzzled me. I just would never leave this book lying around the house where my daughter could find it. And as a teacher I would *never* consider using it in a course!" So then I got into this business about the reason they couldn't get to the book. I told them, it's because of the whole thing of sex being dirty. Because of what St. Paul left to their culture, their western sensibility. And the only person there who came up to me later and said something positive about how I had explained it was a nun. She's not wearing her habit now. She said. "You know, you're right: we are too hungup."

SHEPPERD: Along the line of talking about leaving the books out for the daughters to see them, especially when these days the daughters have probably read them first. Victor's poetry seems to relate directly to what young people can see on the block. Are we reaching a point where we no longer need to append to a page of poetry that it was written by a 14-year-old girl as a rationale for its not meeting certain aesthetic standards? Are we reaching a point where perhaps a 14-year-old girl in the ghetto can capture in her poetry the images that hit us in the gut perhaps even better than did Langston Hughes will all his aesthetic excellence?

MAJOR: I think those standards should really be questioned. I'm doing it myself. I'm really questioning a lot of accepted standards.

CRUZ: I think that a lot of what's happening in American Literature is that people kind of know what to expect. And if somebody from Harlem writes a book they are expected to be a manchild in the promised land. People only really like something when they know exactly what's coming. But I write what I really *want* to do. I'm dealing more with Puerto Rican music and Puerto Rican rhythm and I'm using a lot of chants. I'm relying a lot on religion, the spiritualism that has always been in Caribbean culture. And I'm dealing with the African gods and how people use them, the whole thing of being possessed by spirits. What I'm getting into is getting away from something you see in a lot of black poetry. The thing is, it's much more important to get involved in life and what people are experiencing, because that will be able to stand a lot longer time than an attack which may be over after awhile. Poetry should be creating life instead of using it as some kind of vehicle for some already known object.

MAJOR: Ideally a writer might actually set as a goal the day when he can stop writing.

SHEPPERD: Getting back to what you said about being somewhat uncomfortable running down strictly criticism and interpretation, you mentioned that it was a more meaningful experience to read your work. But doesn't the writer run the risk of being put on the shelf as an entertainer?

MAJOR: One person really got to that at the conference. Most of the participants call me Clarence, but she said, "Mr. Major, I sense in you an uneasiness like we're imposing on you and I don't want to bother you with a whole lot of stupid questions but I know that somehow all of us are missing the point." And this is what she meant, "I don't want to force you to have to perform, to do something you don't want to do because what's going on in you in terms of yourself as a writer is a very private process." Then just for a moment we were quiet and I think we really communicated.

I read my work and that doesn't bother me, but it's afterwards, when people come up to ask dumb questions. Sometimes I can handle it but I don't like to be nasty. Like when I was at the University of Rhode Island. I read sections from *All-Night Visitors*. Afterward a teacher came up and said. "All those four-letter words! It's unbelievable in a school, classroom situation." But, she said, "After the shock wore off, it really became functional, and I saw what you were doing."

CRUZ: The problem I find is that I go to read my poems and they want me to predict the future. Like what's going to happen this summer. And how should I know.

MAJOR: What's happening there is that in this society if you've written a book it makes you an authority on everything.

SHEPPERD: Isn't this also a very subtle racism? People didn't go to Steinbeck and ask him what was going to happen in the ghetto. Isn't is because the ghetto is supposed to be full of illiterates, minority groups are supposed to be stupid and lazy, and here you both have conformed on the white standard of writing a book and getting it published by a major house.

Therefore, you're made the spokesman, just like Richard Wright was made a spokesman, just like Baldwin was made a spokesman, just like Cleaver was made a spokesman.

CRUZ: Right. One cat even asked me about Puerto Ricans in labor unions. They try to make you into something they can understand; then they can go home feeling OK. But with me, they went home without understanding me. And I don't understand myself; because I won't play their game.

SHEPPERD: This gets to a point raised in the conference about the balance in a Black Literature course between art and politics. In a time of social change everyone is pushing, and you as writers must get pushed pretty hard. What kind of relationship do you have to work out between art and politics?

MAJOR: Well, obviously, art is always neglected. Look at a book like Cane, neglected all these years. Even now it's being brought back for the wrong reasons, political rather than aesthetic reasons.

CRUZ: A good example of this is one time I read my poems and I said something about Puerto Rico's flag. Now the flag and all the symbols of the Puerto Rican nationalists are very, very important to them. So afterward one of them came up and said, "Hey, what did you have to say that for?" You know, it shows that in a way all these revolutionary nationalist movements are really very conservative. LeRoi Jones said something about this. He said that the true revolutionary wants to change the culture.

SHEPPERD: In terms of changing the culture, Ishmael Reed seems to be telling us in his work, particularly in his use of Eastern and Egyptian symbolism, that we can participate in this kind of revolution if we change our cutural reference points. What he and Jones before him seem to be saying is

121

that we need a new language. How do you come to grips with this in your work?

MAJOR: I think that we're all suffering from cultural shock and there are a lot of things that won't be clear until we get beyond that. The only thing I trust now is my intuition. The American Communist Party has been telling us for generations that all we have to do to get things straight is to eliminate capitalism. But I think we're seeing that it goes way far beyond that . . .

CRUZ: This is a racist culture and if you want to eliminate racism you have to eliminate the whole culture. Even in Cuba they're having problems because they're approaching problems from a European bag. Latin America shouldn't even be called Latin. It's really Indo-America.

SHEPPERD: Since the novel is a western invention, do we need a new form to express what the new culture will be?

MAJOR: I don't know if the present forms of the novel are worth saving. The word "novel" itself is really totally inappropriate.

CRUZ: I'm trying to work a thing into my readings with singing and Caribbean instruments, like the marracas, the cowbell, the cobassa. If you're ever heard Eddie Palmieri or Ray Barreto you know they have an *after* thing. After one sings, the others come in with something else. It backs you up. This is what I'm trying to do with some people from New York. This, after all, is what Caribbean music is: poetry. In Puerto Rico and Cuba they have street singers who walk the streets singing the blues or singing about happiness. Which in a lot of ways is like an Eastern thing. And this is what I want to get into because this is the way we can tell people to get up and dance. It's the same kind of thing being done by the Temptations. When you get people *into* the lyrics, not just listening to them. A big Latin dance in New York is something a very intellectual dude from Harvard can't understand because he can't catch the sensibility of it. Ray Barreto has a song called *Live and Mess Around*. That's what I want to get to in my poetry. It's like a very rhythmic thing. It's like a tradition, like an ongoing thing.

SHEPPERD: Are these traditions that have been lost in our culture or have they been there all the time, in all sectors of American society?

CRUZ: I don't know what the rest of America is doing but these are things that have been very much kept in black and Puerto Rican neighborhoods and in the mountains, too. It's a music, not a listening music; it's a dance music. If you talked to a group of Puerto Rican teenagers, they'd be talking about the dance steps and how to do them. And that's really where it's at. It's not something you can sit around and talk about. It's something you've got to get up and do: the invitation to the dance.

SHEPPERD: You've both rejected the role of prophets here, saying that you're forced into that role too often, but I'm going to ask you to prophesy just a little. What will we see in the literature of the 70s?

CRUZ: I can only think in terms of what I'm going to be doing. I think that the whole presentation of the writer will change. Like the thing about having a book out. I could dig getting more into leaflets. The writer needs to get more into *his* world, what comes out of his head: feelings and emotions. Actually the only thing we should keep is words. Everything else should break down.

MAJOR: I'd like to pick up on what Victor was saying, particularly about not generalizing. Yesterday Addison Gayle, a consultant to this program, asked me if it bothered me that James Baldwin sees the homosexual crisis as something intrin-

123

sic to the black experience. I told him that it didn't bother me at all because it wasn't—on a personal level—my problem. I mean to say with this example that somehow we're going to have to look at people on a one-at-a-time basis. We can't oversimplify when we're trying to be sincere, real.

Anyway, the future is another thing. I usually refuse to play the game of predicting the future but I can say this—I'd like to do something *new* with the novel. I'd like to do something new with the novel as form. And getting rid of that name would be the first step.

Self Interview: On Craft

Q Major, you write poems, novels, stories, essays and . . . what else? Tell me, *why* do you write?

A I always feel silly trying to answer such questions. Everybody before me who ever tried to deal with this one I'm sure either felt the same way or, if the person attempted to answer, he or she was pretending to know something at a level no one can fully penetrate. I mean, we don't even know *why* we talk. We don't know why we write. All we know is how we do it and that we do have this urge to communicate. It all happens on a level we cannot explain. All we can do is guess and possibly create myths and religions about and around the mystery. I suspect the roots are at the level of being itself. But I can be fairly clear about the type of person I am and that, too, might lend a clue. If I had lived millions of years ago I'd probably be one of the ones drawing pictures on the walls of the cave.

Q Drawing pictures, communicating, you mean, all the same as writing—any kind of communication?

A Yes, but each form has its own material, you know.

Q Speaking of material, what is the material you use for your work?

A It depends on what you mean by material. Literary material in a sense has no real physical property. In one sense, it is only the arrangement of words that the writer can claim. No writer can claim each word or each letter. No manuscript in itself is the ultimate property. The characters in a story are not real people. They cannot be based on real people. They are words and not simply words on paper. What you end with, as a writer, is an investment in a network of ideas and impressions created by tools that belong to the community of man.

Q I know I wasn't very explicit when I said material.

A Well, I use the typewriter and pencils and pens. For longer works I use the typewriter. For poems, very often, I use pens then type the stuff later. What you use and how you use it also determines the shape of what you make. The size of the page, you may be surprised, has a lot to do with the sense of size in the outcome of your poem.

Q What about subject matter?

A Subject matter is usually directly from my own experience. I try to wait until the experience is completely internalized before trying to handle it in terms of art. If I try to write about something that happened recently it usually turns out badly. I have to be emotionally removed to a degree. But, at the same time, if I am too far removed, emotionally, it won't work that way either. It becomes a question of balance—how I handle the interplay between what has gone into my unconscious and what remains controlled at a concious level. And you might say the *ear* and eye participations, the senses, are the mediums through which I allow the plays to be made. By plays I mean the decisions, moment by moment. From letter to letter, and word to word. You see, I have to situate myself between those two poles, trusting them and what they do for and mean for each other. Yet I still have to be involved enough to care. I have to care about my words—the arrangements' effects. They have to mean a lot to me before they take on magical meaning for someone else.

Q But do you write about your own experience directly as it happens?

A No. Never. There is no such thing, really. Something that comes close to passing for that sort of work is journalism but journalism is as much a lie as fiction. All words are lies when they, in any arrangement, pretend to be other than the arrangement they make. On the other hand, what I try to do is achieve a clear and solid mass of arrangements, an entity, that passes for nothing—except flashes of scenes and impressions we all know—much outside the particular, shape of its own "life." Again, the wedding of the conscious and unconscious. Anything I can use I use. Whether or not the material is directly mine from experience I use it if it has meaning for me. If I see a matchbox sitting on the kitchen table, while I'm typing, I might just stick it into the story I'm working on. See. Or, if I hear something on the radio, while I'm sitting at the typewriter typing a novel, I might just throw in a news report as I hear it, perhaps changing some of it to make it work into the novel. I do anything that works. I open my mind and make it completely—well, as completely as possible—accessible to everything and anything that comes into the circle of my senses or memory or personal space or all of these at the same time. Of course this does not mean that it is by any means possible to record everything. You snatch away from the whole mass of stuff only a tiny portion and it gives you the suggestion for some of the substance that goes into what you're doing, be it a novel or poem or whathaveyou. Direct or indirect it is all my experience. If I simply read a book it becomes *my* experience.

Q Do you value *all* elements of your own experience—as material for fiction or poetry?

A No, definitely not. I try to rely on a sort of unconscious screening device or selector. I try to let the feeling (somewhere behind the mind that guides the front part of the mind) determine everything. If I am lucky it happens successfully; if not, I have to try again.

Q Then you write purely from feeling?

A Not purely. It is thick with many other juices. It also has in it the substance of uncertainty and, on occasion, a touch of the ego. And selfishness at its worst. But no one can write purely from feeling; it has to be a mixture of many and different motives and means and ends. All of which calls into question who and what we are. Any one of us at any given moment.

Q Do you ever find yourself unable to write?

A Not really. Usually I *can* write *something*. I might not be able to write as well as I'd like to write all the time but just writing something, anything, is always easy. And it is not uncommon for the best poem or story to come out of a mood and state of mind that are cool and, perhaps, even a little turned off.

Q What is the degree of your concern with artistic quality in your work?

A It occupies a large part of my overall concern. Because I'd like to turn out top-rate stuff all the time. The thing I hate worse than anything else is to spend six months on a novel and have it turn out a turd. It can easily happen. But I can usually salvage most of my failures. But the artistic quality itself, for me, is the first consideration. It comes before shit like "message" and such jive. A lot of black writers tend to get hungup in militant rhetoric, thinking they can save their people. The deliberate effort, propaganda, has never helped anyone toward a larger sense of self. It has always been the novel or poem that begins from and spreads all across the entire human experience that ends liberating minds. These militant fictionists, hungup in their slogans and dialect-writing, are simply competing with newspapers and the six o'clock news and house organs and cheap politicians. Apparently they never once stop to think about the artistic quality of their work, mainly, I guess, because white folks never told them it applied to them. And, by the way, I'm not talking about artistic standards based on European-American concepts of excellence. Rather, I'm referring to formative and functional standards that have their origins in African cultures. Aside from the most obvious uses of art, it is supposed to help deepen and widen one's sense and vision of life. Anyway, I don't want to get into all this too deeply . . . I've heard myself say it too many times.

128

Q Tell me, Major, (that is, if I may ask) do you make a living from your writing?

A Most of the time. When I don't, I teach writing or literature to supplement my income.

Q Do you like teaching?

A I don't particularly like teaching but I like working with students *if* they're interested in what is going on.

Q I see. But let us get back to your own writing. Exactly how do you go about writing a novel? Do you use charts? Do you make a list of the characters first? Do you begin with an outline or . . .

A It all depends on the novel. I wrote *All-Night Visitors* casually over a period of four years. I used bits and parts of other discarded works. Some parts of it were written many times over and other parts went in the final draft without any alterations from the original draft. It was originally a very ambitious book that got a lot of its life knocked out of it by its publisher, Maurice Girodias, who wanted it cut—and I cut it—to fit the format of hardcover books he was trying to publish at that time. Regarding how I worked on it, yes, I used charts and lists of names and everything I could get my hands on. I read a dictionary of the slang used by U.S. military men in Vietnam. I even worked some of my poems into the action.

Q What about *NO*?

A With *NO* the situation was altogether different. The first draft was done on teletype paper fed into the typewriter from a spool I made myself. I finished the first draft in, I think, about two months of very casual work. The second and final draft, done on regular typing paper, was done in about the same length of time. I finished *NO* in the fall of 1969.

Q Do you want also to talk about *Reflex and Bone Structure*?

A I certainly do not.

Q Why not?

A It is a question of time.

Q All right, good enough. How about your poetry. How is it done? Can you talk about it?

A Some of it is very personal and comes straight out of that kind of reference. Other poems are suggested by any number of things or situations. As I said earlier, I use anything I can lay my hands on. The only criterion is it *must* work. The impetus might even be something like the patterns in this rug here on the floor at this moment. They may suggest something, an idea that begins and expands, growing into a complex network of stuff. I like to think of the growth as organic—that is, in a sense, organic. Anything. The fish over there in the fishtank. Anything at all.

Q Then, how do you know how to direct all of this once it begins?

A It's simple. It builds itself, like a snowball. Or see it as crust, like the outside of cake.

Q Crust?

A Yes. In a sense, the stuff that is excess to the original idea . . . *Certainly you must know what I mean!* All of this seems, to me, so obvious!

Q What about the creative process?

A Well, what about it?

Q Can you tell me something about it?

A No, I doubt it.

Q Your nonfiction. Does it differ in conception and process from your fiction and poetry?

A Only on the surface, I think. With polemics, you know, there is the uppermost point of a *message*. It is the center of the universe of nonfiction. Whereas, on the other hand, in a novel or a poem, you may simply be concerned with producing a drama of an aspect of life or all of life. Personally, I like fiction and poetry better. Nonfiction, due to the influence of the times I guess, I enjoy reading.

Q Do you mean *The New York Times?*

A That, my friend, was gutty!

Q Gutty? Well, I won't worry about it. Can you answer a few more questions?

A No more questions, my friend.
Q Not even one?
A Not one.

Interview with Clarence Major

This interview was conducted by John O'Brien for use in his book, Interviews With Black Writers, (Liveright) 1973.

INTERVIEWER: In your essay "A Black Criteria" you call for black writers to break away from Westernized literary strictures. Do you think of *All-Night Visitors* as being an example of a "non-Western" novel?

MAJOR: I've changed since writing that essay in 1967. I now find repulsive the idea of calling for black writers to do anything other than what they each choose to do. A lot of blacks grew up in the United States and became writers. They are different because of the racial climate and because of this country's history, but they still are part of this common American experience. They may speak black English and use Afro-American slang, and eat black-eyed peas and corn bread, yet they are not African. And certainly they are not Chinese. So what do we have? We are Americans. We work in English; it may be black English, but at its roots it's English. This does not mean that there are not several unique black writers. If you look at Cecil Brown, Al Young, William Demby, Ron Fair and Charles Wright, you'll see how original the contemporary black fictionist really is. But as far as some kind of all-encompassing black aesthetic is concerned, I don't think black writers can be thrown together like that into some kind

133

of formula. Black writers today should write whatever they want to write and in any way they choose to write it. No style or subject should be alien to them. We have to get away from this rigid notion that there are certain topics and methods reserved for black writers. I'm against all that. I'm against coercion from blacks and from whites.

INTERVIEWER: Then you did not intend that your first novel be seen as working against a Western idea of what the novel should be?

MAJOR: No. *All-Night Visitors* was not a non-Western novel. I was struggling against a lot of Western concepts when I wrote it, but it is still an American novel. I once said that it was not a Christian novel. Christianity is something with which I have been at war almost all my life. When I was a kid I believed the things I was told about God and the devil. I think that in the West Christianity's great attraction is that it offers life after death. It's something that people can lose themselves in because they can say that everything is going to be all right. Eastern religions don't have that built-in escape nor do they have the tremendous self-hatred that's at the center of Christianity. These feelings about Christianity are in my work because I agonized with this things in my own experience of growing up, these problems of good and evil and sex. I think that's why there's so much sex in *All-Night Visitors*. Here was a man who could express himself only in this one natural way because he had absolutely nothing else. Christianity's view toward sex exists because of the great self-hatred that's so embedded in Christian teaching. Look at St. Paul's doctrine of Original Sin. I can see it in everything around us: sex is something that's nasty and something to hide. *All-Night Visitors* was a novel I had to write in order to come to terms with my own body. I also wanted to deal with the other body functions. In *NO* I was trying to exploit all the most sacred taboos in this culture, not just sexual taboos, but those related to the private functions of the body and that's where they all seem to center.

INTERVIEWER: Sex in *All-Night Visitors* is used in many ways. As you say, it is the only means that Eli Bolton has of expressing himself. But it also reminds Eli of death and is sometimes quite violent and brutal. At the same time I don't think that sex is used in a metaphorical way for implying the changes that Eli undergoes.

MAJOR: Eli's attitudes about sex reflect the crisis of the 1960's. In speaking of the novel John A. Williams said that it is a sad book that gives off a kind of gentle helplessness and anger with no place to go and that it shows the discontent of the "death-wait" in our society. Now, sex features very large in *All-Night Visitors* and so does violence. I wanted it that way because this society is preoccupied with both. All kinds of negative stigmas concerning sex have been imposed on black men by both black and white people. And Eli doesn't escape this kind of psychological warfare. Some people feel that by showing Eli's sex life I'm playing right into the hands of white myths about black people. And white liberals have expressed pretty much the same sort of reaction to the novel. All I can say it that certain people have no interest in the human body and even hate it. These people seem to have no sex life.

INTERVIEWER: Why does Eli see the relationship between sex and death?

MAJOR: When you ask about sex and death in the same breath you really hit on something in the book, something most people concerned with the sexual aspect of the book never get to. Any fiction that tries to deal with sex in an open and honest way and attempts to get beneath the purely physical is bound to come to terms with the link between sex and death. I don't mean that sex is here at the beginning and death there at the end. They are interchangeable. The expression of one can be found in the act of the other. I think that the French word for orgasm can be translated "little death." And I think that you are right when you observe that sex isn't meant to

135

correspond with anything that Eli's going through. It is rather a kind of alternative to the brutality around him. That's one of the last natural things he has in a world where he cannot assert himself. It is a means of expression and, at times, a weapon.

INTERVIEWER: Eli keeps complaining about how "unreal" the world about him has become. I wonder whether his search for some new reality, which begins with discarding old sexual myths, requires that he question all the "realities" that his culture lives by? And perhaps it calls into question what the author's relationship with reality is. Does he reflect it, as the traditional realist supposedly does, or does he invent it, as the fantasy novel, begun by Sterne, does?

MAJOR: I really don't like either idea. The novel is an invention in itself which exists on its own terms. It has its own reality and I don't think it's designed to reflect reality in any kind of logical sense. It's not a way of showing reality and it's not really a fantasy. But then I'm simply talking about what the novel means to me. The kind of novel that I'm concerned with writing is one that takes on its own reality and is really independent of anything outside itself.

INTERVIEWER: In some very real practical sense, though, a writer is forced into relating himself to the outside world. He may choose to ignore it or try to see it in a new way in his fiction, but he must always be reacting to it in some way.

MAJOR: But in a novel the only thing you really have is words. You begin with words and you end with words. The content exists in our minds. I don't think that it has to be a reflection of anything. It is reality that has been created inside of a book. It's put together and exists finally in your mind. I don't want to say that a novel is *totally* independent from the reality of things in everyday life, but it's not the same thing. It's certainly not the kind of reflection that's suggested by the metaphor of the mirror.

INTERVIEWER: Well, I think that you are subscribing to this tradition of the fantasy novel. Rather than life, it uses the imagination and the novel itself as its primary subject.

MAJOR: Its subject matter is the novel itself? Yes. I think that's closer to the truth. At the same time I know that my fiction has been directly influenced by other things. I regret, for instance, in my haphazard education my exposure to Freudian psychology because it has left its effect in my thinking. Since I finished *NO* I found myself weeding out so much of it. I can't reject it all because we live in a technological world where we have certain ways of dealing with reality. But that's one thing that I regret about *NO*. I noticed the Freudian influence there and it's very disturbing. That whole sensibility is probably present in my earlier work too, and it's a sensibility that I want to forget. I don't want to get trapped in terminology. I worry that, despite the fact that *NO* came from the gut level, a large part of it seems to be caught in the sensibility of Freudian psychology.

INTERVIEWER: One might also question what psychology's relation to reality is.

MAJOR: I think that you should stop when you use the word "reality" because reality itself is very flexible and really has nothing to do with anything. I don't think that reality is a fixed point that theories adjust around. Reality is anything but a fixed point. So, it seems strange to me that a work of art could be an interpretation of *the* reality.

INTERVIEWER: I agree with that, but we usually do not take that approach to a system like psychology which is really just as fictional as literature. Psychology is only an attempt to impose an artificial order on the chaos, but the chaos remains. In literature we most often make a distinction between it as an imaginative act and as a truthful picture of the way things are. But we don't make that distinction with philosophy or psychology which really has no relation to anything except

137

itself. I agree with you that reality is no fixed point, yet some-one like Freud imposes his pattern and says, "Here it is. Here is the truth." Perhaps we should look at psychology as essentially an imaginative act.

MAJOR: Yes, right. You're absolutely right. Freud was inventing. He was doing the same thing a novelist would do. He was creating his own reality. It was an invention just like Darwin's, despite the correspondences to what we call "facts." They are still inventions. That may have something to do with the nature of writing and thinking, thoughts relating to words.

INTERVIEWER: I see so much of your fiction as an attempt to break away from the myths that men have invented which now tyrannize them. Sometimes those myths are Christian ones, sometimes psychological, and sometimes racial. I see very much the same thing going on in Ishmael Reed's fiction and Michael Harper's poetry.

MAJOR: I see them in Ishmael's work. He was exposed to pretty much the same kind of background that I was. He handles this in a different way; we all do. And it isn't just Christianity in my work. There's the whole racial thing which I try to handle not as a psychologist or a sociologist but as a writer who tries to integrate these things into a novel. This, by the way, is what I have against a lot of black fiction. So much seems designed to preach racial or political or sociological sermons.

INTERVIEWER: At one point in *All-Night Visitors* Eli reflects that " I suppose we have all gotten used to it. Our dislocation is so complete." Do you think that the unifying theme of the novel is the various forms of dislocation Eli experiences?

MAJOR: Yes, I'd agree with you that the dislocation can serve as a kind of unifying theme. I like the sense that you get from the novel. Not many people came away from it with the feeling that the story, if I can say story, is a nightmare in which a whole series of strange things happen. But that was the impression I wanted to create.

INTERVIEWER: In the "Basement Rite" chapter you slip into a surrealistic style. It's interesting because the story up to this point has been very bizarre, but it isn't until this chapter that you break away from a naturalistic treatment of your materials. When it occurs one hardly notices the shift in style because it seems like such a logical extension of what's been going on.

MAJOR: Real and surreal are two tricky words, but I know what you mean. I can't think of a term at the moment that would be better. The entire novel is meant to have that surreal quality. Many people, unfortunately, missed this in the book because, I suppose, they were too concerned with the surface reality.

INTERVIEWER: Why was the novel written in rather short episodic chapter? There's really little or no plot. Were you purposely breaking away from the traditional realistic narrative?

MAJOR: I discovered early that what I was trying to do in *All-Night Visitors* could not be done in a smooth symphonic fashion. I needed short broken chapters, little twisted episodes. Omitting traditional plot and other kinds of traditional devices was dictated by the same need to capture all the elements of this "unreal world" into a form specifically designed for it.

INTERVIEWER: What went into structuring these episodes?

MAJOR: The arrangement of the chapters changed quite a bit in the several drafts preceeding the final one. I followed my feelings with very little conscious planning. In other words, the writing itself was the discovery of what the novel was.

INTERVIEWER: Unlike the rest of the novel, there's a lyrical spirit in the chapter "Week-End Away." It seems to clash with the tone of the novel and to suggest certain qualities about the character of Eli that are not present in the other chapters.

MAJOR: What Eli feels and expressess in that chapter is very real. He would be a quiet peaceful person if his world permitted him to be. That chapter is one of my favorite in the book. I think it shows a side to Eli that one has to see in order to undestand the other sides.

INTERVIEWER: The novel ends with Eli helping a destitute Spanish family, and he feels that "I had become firmly a man." I am not sure how seriously to take all this, whether or not to believe that a change has taken place. All the evil that he has seen and felt does not seem to be balanced by this one moment of light.

MAJOR: No one ever says, "Now I have become a man." That moment is never so clear. It happens slowly and in so many unseen ways that there isn't likely to be a moment as dramatic as the one Eli experiences. I had him stand in a doorway, with rain failing, thinking this. It works all right in a novel, but I am not so sure that it works as well in what we call reality. One person told me that she did not believe the ending. It was not credible that he could have given his apartment to a helpless woman and her children. Others have felt that the ending explained everything and gave the novel its point. Yet, I wasn't trying to make any point when I wrote the novel. I was simply trying to describe Eli's life and what it was like for a black man in the 1960s. Ron Welburn in *The Nickel Review* said that the book had no overt message. That was the way I wanted it because Eli's life really had no point.

INTERVIEWER: One recurring concern in both novels is that of the "self." One way of looking at your characters is that they lack a sense of who they are and they must discover that. But looked at in the way I think you intend it to be, the self is really a non-existing thing or something that is in a constant state of becoming. Moses in *NO,* for instance, is all the things that happen to him and all the ways that people look at him. In this sense, one cannot say that his problem is that he doesn't know who he is. The point is that he isn't one thing but many. Is the self something that is created rather than found or uncovered?

MAJOR: The notion of self in *NO* is dealt with in a superficial way. The narrator says at various times that he thinks that the idea of a self is ridiculous. He's called by many names. This might be a clue to just how artificial or shifting this whole business of self becomes. (The search for freedom is another artificial thing in the novel that's deliberately artificial. There's no such thing as freedom in the sense in which it's used in that novel.) At one point he's called Nicodemus, which is something out of Negro folklore. And he's called C. C. Rider.

INTERVIEWER: And at times "the Boy."

MAJOR: Right. And Ladykiller, the Inspector, and June Bug. And there's a play on Nat Turner; the narrator is called Nat Turnips. And, of course, the name he usually goes by is Moses. Did you get the sense that there were two Moses?

INTERVIEWER: Yes. One is the narrator and the other is this father figure.

MAJOR: One is definitely the father image. And although it wouldn't be the wisest thing to do, you could substitute "God" for "father." It wouldn't be too far off either . . . But to get back to your question about the notion of self. I was trying to show all the shifting elements of the so-called self. One way that I did it was by giving the narrator all these names. The other Moses, of course, is not concerned with problems of who he is. He's a doer, he's a hard hitting, physical type;

the narrator is more reflective and spiritual. The father is really the "ladykiller."

INTERVIEWER: Yes, literally.

MAJOR: He's a sort of pimp and he's a hustler. He's deadly and yet he's gentle. I tried to make his character difficult to penetrate.

INTERVIEWER: I wanted to ask you about the bullfight scene at the end of the novel in relation to this question of the self. Does it suggest something along the lines of the Hemingway idea of the moment of truth?

MAJOR: I hope that it's not that corny, but it may be.

INTERVIEWER: What is it that happens there? Must he have this encounter with death before he can be free of these terrible things in his past?

MAJOR: He must come to terms with an ultimate act. He has to have that look into the endless horror of things in order to get beyond the whole petty business of worrying about it.

INTERVIEWER: I wonder why you did not write *NO* as a naturalistic novel. In some ways it is merely a story of a boy growing up.

MAJOR: Why do you think that he is young?

INTERVIEWER: I assumed that he was now looking back on the things that happened to him as a boy.

MAJOR: Right. That's what I was trying to do. I was trying not only to construct a chronological story but one that was psychologically unrestricted by time. You notice that there are elements from the 1920s, the 1930s, and the 1940s. And there are qualities out of the 1970s and the space age. I was trying to bring all of this together and blend them into a kind of consciousness that was not restricted. I wanted a landscape in language that would give me the freedom to do this. I felt that this freedom could not be achieved in a naturalistic novel.

INTERVIEWER: Yes. You would not have had the range you needed. You move through all different states of mind and ages. The narrator not only sees the action and events of the story the way a child would but also as a grown man reflecting on and shaping those experiences.

MAJOR: You also probably noticed that I was grabbing at every useful reference that I could get my hands on: magic, mysticism, Judeo-Christian religion, philosophy, witchcraft, American superstition and folklore, black terminology, and black slang. But I didn't start out with any conscious notion of doing that; it just developed in a very organic way. It was only after I finished the first draft that I saw what I wanted to do. When I got that finished I started making out elaborate charts with the names of the characters, personality sketches, and their possible ages. I worked hard at inventing names that would really work with the characters, names like Grady Flower, Lucy Nasteylip, Grew, and B.B. B.B. is a name that little black boys in the South are often given.

INTERVIEWER: There are many Southern elements in the novel. At times I was reminded of Faulkner.

MAJOR: It's very definitely a Southern novel. I tried to capture the flavor of the South as I remember it. There was also a subdued treatment of the relationship between the country and the city, but it wasn't fully developed in the novel. The paradox of the country and the city is very deep in me because I know both. I was born in the city but shortly after that I lived in the country. It's been that way on and off ever since.

INTERVIEWER: Was it difficult getting through the first draft of *NO*?

MAJOR: What I am doing right now is to outline a novel

very consciously and it's very difficult because I am watching too closely what I am doing. I didn't have that problem with *NO*. With *NO* I got teletype paper, put it on a spool and made a little platform with a stick, adjusted the typewriter, and I sent the paper into the typewriter and wrote it on this endless sheet of paper. It was a very spontaneous thing. I would write until I ran out of steam. It was very easy to do because it was a story that I had been trying to write since I was twelve. It was the story I needed to write most. I wrote it in 1969 when my personal life was really tossed around in many ways. But I had finally reached the point where I felt that I could finally do it. Although it's not an autobiographical novel, its roots are very deep in my emotional life. So, though it's fictional in its design, the energy that holds it together is very real. This is true of any fiction.

INTERVIEWER: You and I have talked before about the relationship between your poetry and your fiction. What do you see as the relationship between the two?

MAJOR: Much of my poetry is purely fictional. I sincerely believe good poetry should be fictional. I work hard to make all my poems work as fiction. My newest book of poems, which hasn't been published yet, *The Syncopated Cakewalk,* is pure fiction. I think that it was Carson McCullers who said that poetry should be more like fiction and that fiction should be more like poetry. I am working very deliberately to break down what I think are the false distinctions between poetry and fiction.

INTERVIEWER: Is there an essential difference, though, that still exists? Does it have to do with the use of language or that fiction is still narrative in nature?

MAJOR: No, I don't see the difference. But I am really in a state of transition with all of this. It is rather dfficult for me to abstract theories about what this means and where I'm going with it.

INTERVIEWER: I know that you attended the Art Institute in Chicago for a while. Has painting affected your writing in any way?

MAJOR: The Art Institute experience has often been misunderstood. It didn't involve any academic classes. I was there on a fellowship to sketch and paint. I learned a lot in those days, but mainly on my own, upstairs in the gallery and in the library. I was very serious about painting. I almost painted my mother out of house and home actually. We nearly ran out of space, but my mother always encouraged me to paint. She wanted me to become a painter. I think my experience with painting, the way that I learned to see the physical world of lines, color, and composition, definitely influenced my writing.

INTERVIEWER: Can you describe your work habits?

MAJOR: They change all the time because they depend on the thing I'm doing. If I'm writing a group of short stories, I might work exclusively on one each day. If I'm writing a series of poems I might do one or two a day.

INTERVIEWER: How much revision do you do?

MAJOR: I revise endlessly. Even after publication. I am not one of those writers who sees publication as a cut-off point.

INTERVIEWER: Eli in *All-Night Visitors* says something very interesting and I wonder whether or not it describes your reasons for writing: "the universe is not *ordered,* therefore I am simply pricking the shape of a particular construct, a form, in it." .

MAJOR: I don't know. I suppose writing comes from the need to shape one's experience and ideas. Maybe it assures us a future and a past. We try to drive away our fears and uncertainties and explain the mystery of life and the world.

Black Criteria

The black poet confronted with western culture and civilization must isolate and define himself in as bold a relief as he is capable of. He must chop away at the white criterion and destroy its hold on his black mind because seeing the world through white eyes from a black soul causes death. The black poet must not attempt to create from a depth of black death. The true energy of black art must be brought fully into the possession of the black creator. The black poet must stretch his consciousness not only in the direction of other non-western people across the earth, but in terms of pure "reason" as well, and must expand the mind-areas to the far reaches of creativity's endlessness to fiind new ways of seeing the world the black poet of the west is caught up in.

If we black poets see ourselves and our relationship with the deeper elements of life and with all mankind, perhaps we can also break through the tangled ugly white energy of western fear and crime. We are in a position to know at first hand the social and political machinery that is threatening to destroy the earth, and we can use a creative and intellectual black criteria on it.

I believe the artist does owe something to the society in which he is involved; he should be involved fully. This is the measure of the poet, and the black poet in his—if you notice how white people see us—invisibility must hammer away at his own world of creative criticism of this society. A work of art, a poem, can be a complete "thing"; it can be alone, not preaching, not trying to change men, and though it might change them, if the men are ready for it, the poem is not reduced in its artistic status. I mean we black poets can write poems of pure creative black energy right here in the white west and make them works of art without falling into the cheap market place of bullshit and propaganda. But it is a thin line to stand on.

We are the "eye" of the west really.

We must shake up not only our own black brothers but also the superficial and shoddy people stumbling in the brainlessness of the western decline. We must use our black poetic energy to overthrow the western ritual and passion, the curse, the dark ages of this death, the original sin's impact on a people and their unjust projection of it upon us black people; we must lead ourselves out of this madness and if our journey brings out others—perhaps even white people—then it will be good for us all. We must use our magic!

The nightmare of this western sadism must be fought with a superior energy, and black poetic spirits are powerful weapons!

With the poem, we must erect a spiritual black nation we all can be proud of. And at the same time we must try to do the impossible—always the impossible—by bringing the poem back into the network of man's social and political life.

Total life is what we want.

On Censorship:
An Open Letter
To June Jordan

March 5, 1973
New York, N.Y.

Dear June:

I mentioned it before: Jane Cooper told me about your novel, *His Own Where,* being banned in Maryland. I am not surprised; not even the reason surprises me. Though at first I
thought—before I knew the reason—it might be due to the
love-sexual scene in the graveyard. Your note explains: "The
ban—Black English allegedly bad influence of Black children
who need to learn standard English." Aside from the fact that
images of self in our own rhythms, syntax, slang, and feelings
are very healthy and necessary, the position taken against
your book is pathetic. On February 8, this year, at the New
School, I listened to a panel of three people discuss literature
and revolution. They were Francine Du Plessix Gray, Jerzy
Kozinski and Anthony Burgess. Burgess, in his high-handed
manner, dismissed Black English as a deprived and dangerous
tongue. What he meant by dangerous is anybody's guess. Further, he suggested that James Baldwin was the only good black
writer. In connection with this, he mentioned the fact that
Baldwin's work shows the influence of Henry James.

But I want to tell you of my own ups and downs with censorship. For whatever it is worth we need to keep each other informed on such matters. If we let things slide, the ones against freedom of expression may have their way.

An incident enough related to censorship to deserve space here took place in 1968 while I was putting together my anthology, *The New Black Poetry*. Ed Spriggs, a black poet, launched a boycott against the projected book on the grounds that it was being published by a white company. I'd called Spriggs and asked for poems, telling him about the project and who would publish the anthology. At first he agreed to contribute, then approached a second time for the poems he had not sent, he refused. It was not yet clear why. In the fall of 1968 the *Journal of Black Poetry* carried Spriggs' explanation. In part it said: "me? i'm nuttin on every thing directed to the mother country's houses that shld and cld be published black ..." Aside from the fact that I had, long before 1968, published my work through black and other outlets I was not then, am not now, a nationalist. It was Spriggs' position. My position is simple: I am against restrictions, oppression, repression, and censorship. The irony of course is I believe in boycotts. Especially effective boycotts for good reasons. I am against coercion and for freedom of choice. I would demonstrate for the right of nationalists to be nationalists but I insist on my right not to be one. To illustrate the principle further: to *force* a person to vote is as bad as witholding that right. Anyway not long after this incident Spriggs had poetry appear in an anthology published by William Morrow & Company, Inc., a white-owned and operated house. New American Library publishes Signet books, right? Well in 1971 Spriggs penned the preface to their *Black Dimensions in Contemporary American Art*. He is of course director of the partly white-funded Studio Museum in Harlem. A fine place. In fact Spriggs himself is a fine person. I understand he recently toured Europe to see its museums.

But to return to the specific problem of censorship. During the Metropolitan Museum's 1969 "Harlem On My Mind" show, *The New Black Poetry*—now published and one of the bestselling books on display there—ran into trouble. It was removed by the museum director because *Combat,* a rightist publication, complained about its publisher, International, being a communist outfit. Not only the publisher but some other people reacted with outrage—and rightly so—at the gall of the museum-keeper's removal of the book. Shortly after this the director claims he put the anthology back on display for sale. But no one who went there could find it.

That same year, in December, for two weeks I was visiting writer at the University of Wisconsin at Eau Claire. *All-Night Visitors,* my first novel, was on sale in the school bookstore. That is, until someone complained about the sex in it. Instantly the book was hidden under the counter. Perhaps they thought it would go away. Only after pressure from one person in the English Department did they place it back.

On February 9, 1972, *The Connecticut Western* announced that I, an "Award Winning Black Writer," would "Visit area Schools." At Housatonic Valley Regional High School, Falls Village, Connecticut, on February 17, I read a group of my poems to about 200 people. The reading was open to the public. Among the poems read was "American Setup," which appears in the Random House anthology, *In A Time of Revolution.* After the poem was read Mrs. Joan W. Johnson, of Canaan, walked out with her children in the middle of the next poem. She wrote a letter to *The Lakeville Journal.* It appeared February 24. In part it said, "I sat with my 14-year old son and listened to 'unpublished' poems being read to an audience of an assortment of ages, and was throughly disgusted and shocked by what I was hearing. The filthy language, filth, itself as far as in relation of a poem was abhorrent! . . . Several people around me got up and left, therefore I don't feel I was the only one with these feelings. I sat there becoming angrier by the minute at what I was hearing . . . My daughter stayed on . . ."

In the weeks that followed, *The Connecticut Western* and

151

The Lakeville Journal carried a series of letters from local citizens debating the value of my poetry and what I had done. The videotape of the reading was stolen and a distorted version of the poem written for it and circulated by those responding to Mrs. Johnson's call. A meeting of parents, the press and teachers was called. The videotape was recovered and they all would see it together. My dear friend, Bill DeVoti, director of the poetry program there, would not show the thing except at a meeting open to the public. The principal of the school had requested a private showing. But Bill got his way. And people left the meeting and showing in disagreement. Some agreed that the poem in question *was* obscene, others did not. One reporter felt that Mrs. Johnson was really reacting to the "political" position taken in the poem. All of this, step by step, was reported faithfully in the local news. The headlines ran, "Dirty Poetry," "Clarence Major's Dirty Poetry," "The Debate over Clarence Major's Poetry," "Poems or Porn: Very Much A Question of Today," "Meeting at Regional Probes Poet's Use of Street Language," "A Minor Issue over Mr. Major," "Dirty Poetry in School," on and on. The last article on the incident appeared in *The Connecticut Western* on April 26. Three months! Three months in which the newspapers carried stories and letters expressing a variety of positions. Yet do you think the people learned anything from the incident? I think my friend Bill would say yes.

But it doesn't end here. In December 1972 Mark Mirsky, Faith Sale, Jane Delynn, several other editors of *Fiction,* and I met Walter James Miller at the Municipal Building at Chambers and Center. Purpose: to tape for the WNYC radio show, "Reader's Almanac." Jane Delynn and I did a 30 minute show together. She read a story of her own from *Fiction.* I read my story. "Early Grave," also originally published in *Fiction.* The show was scheduled to go on the air January 14, 1973. It did not. Reason? "Dirty" words. Miller, in a phone conversation, later told me the program director was worried about the Federal Communications Commission. He was also possibly worried about losing his job if the FCC authorities had heard those "dirty" words. Both Delynn and I said words like "fuck" and "shit" just as they appeared in our work. Believe me, none of the revolutions have been won!

Yours,
Clarence